A
PHILOSOPHER'S
NOTES

PRAISE FOR
A PHILOSOPHER'S NOTES

"Brian Johnson has written a wonderful book on optimal living that is very easy to read and has invaluable suggestions on how to live authentic, successful, loving, and happy lives. There is great wisdom in this book to help enrich anyone's life no matter what their age. I wish this book was available 40 years ago when I was just starting out on my own life journey. I whole heartedly recommend it."
— John Mackey, CEO, Whole Foods

"Brilliant! Brian Johnson has a rare gift for fresh-squeezing timeless wisdom and serving it up with a grin. Every single page of this phenomenal little book is packed with life-changing insights and down-to-earth charm. Prepare to get smarter, healthier and happier from the moment you pick it up!"
— Pilar Gerasimo, Editor in Chief of *Experience Life Magazine*

"As a man who's invested better than twenty years inspiring people to lift heavy things to live stronger, it's unsettlingly refreshing to have something so small lift me up and make me stronger and wiser. Brian has mastered the skill of creating "concentrated wisdom" that gives you more freedom, energy and clarity per second than any thing you can do, be or read. I love this book!! Thank you Bri!"
— Shawn Phillips, bestselling lifestyle fitness author, *Strength for LIFE* and Gold Star Practice Contributor to *Integral Life Practice*

"A great resource to live life at your absolute best."
— Robin Sharma, author of the #1 international bestseller
The Leader Who Had No Title

"The little book in your hands will save you big amounts of time, energy and money. How? Brian Johnson has spent years scouring metric tons of publications and figured out what really works so you don't have to. The result? He's made the path to optimal living fun and simple for the rest of us. What more could you ask for?"

— Tripp Lanier, host of The New Man Podcast

"Brian's passionate love of wisdom oozes from A Philosopher's Notes. It's infectious. Distilling ancient wisdom to its essence, A Philosopher's Notes cuts through the noise of uncertainty. Without a wasted word Brian brings modern-world relevance to often-ambiguous philosophical writing, making it accessible and relevant to us all. It truly is the modern-day guide to optimal living."

— Brendan Brazier, bestselling author of *Thrive* and formulator of Vega

"You know how amazing lemon essence is? In a single drop, a whole orchard of lemon brilliance. That's what Brian Johnson is to wisdom. He's taken the best from the best and distilled it down to something that's pure, punchy and practical. A Philosopher's Notes is like an entire library on the secret to your Great Work in the palm of your hand."

— Michael Bungay Stanier, author of *Do More Great Work*

"Brian is a master learner, synthesizer and Creator! This book holds more wisdom than most of us absorb in a lifetime. What a great place to start on the journey — or to use as a "check point" along the way. Thanks, Brian, for your contribution to conscious evolution!"

— David Emerald, author of *The Power of TED**

"Curiosity can kill cats but it can also create cool cats and Brian Johnson is, no doubt, the coolest cat I know. If I could install a "chip" in Chip's head that allowed me to download this book all day long, I'd do it in a minute. Or maybe not, because one of the brilliant truths of A Philosopher's Notes *is the visceral sense of discovery you experience each time you turn the page. These notes are more than streams, they are raging rivers of wisdom and reading just a half dozen pages at a time will sustain you for a week."*
— Chip Conley, founder of Joie de Vivre Hotels and author of
PEAK and *Emotional Equations*

"Imagine if there was a book about personal growth that captured all the great lessons of all the hundreds of other great books and teachers? Look no further, this is the book! A Philosopher's Notes *reads as quick as a page-turning novel, yet is filled with great nuggets of wisdom. Johnson makes every word count but does so with wit and style. Whether you've read 'em all or are new to the self-help aisle,* A Philosopher's Notes *is a must-read. It's one of, if not the best I've read (and I've read a lot of them). Already excited for number two."*
— Jason Wachob, creator of MindBodyGreen.com

"Brian Johnson sees life as a great work-in-progress and each of us as an aspiring artist. With cultivation and practice, we create a masterpiece with and through our lives. Brian's insights, stories, and living example inspire us to fulfill our purpose and potential, and to create an awesome life — for ourselves and those around us!"
— Jeff Klein, author of *Working for Good: Making a Difference While Making a Living*

A
PHILOSOPHER'S
NOTES

:: VOLUME I ::

BRIAN JOHNSON

Published by en*theos Enterprises
18030 Brookhurst Street #334
Fountain Valley, CA 92708
http://entheos.me

Editorial: Jacquelyn B. Fletcher
Cover & Typography: Brian Donahue and Rasheeda Mickel
Cover Illustration: Brian Johnson
Author Photograph: Tim Van Orden

Library of Congress Cataloging-in-Publication Data
Johnson, Brian, 1974— A philosopher's notes on
optimal living, creating an authentically awesome life
and other such goodness.

ISBN 10: 0-9830591-0-1
ISBN 13: 978-0-9830591-0-3

Printed in Canada

Mixed Sources
Product group from well-managed forests,
controlled sources and recycled wood or fiber
www.fsc.org   Cert no. SW-COC-000952
© 1996 Forest Stewardship Council
FSC

*I dedicate this book to all the other Lovers of Wisdom
out there. You inspire me!*

*And, to Alexandra—my Goddess, best friend, soul mate and Wife.
Rubbing feet with you as I wake up in the morning
is one of my greatest joys. I feel so blessed to celebrate our
lives together. Thank you for sharing my enthusiasm for
this book and all of my ideas. I love you. Muah. :)*

CONTENTS

AN INTRO

OPTIMISM

PURPOSE & SELF-AWARENESS

GOALS

ACTION

ENERGY

WISDOM

COURAGE

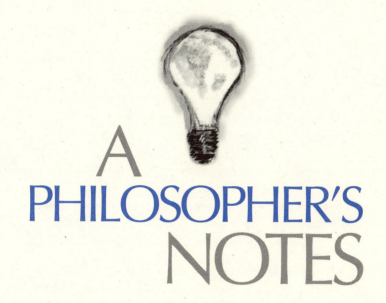

A
PHILOSOPHER'S
NOTES

"This is my way; where is yours?—
Thus I answered those who asked me 'the way.'
For the way—that does not exist."
— Friedrich Nietzsche

"I believe that a life of integrity is the most fundamental source of
personal worth. I do not agree with the popular success
literature that says that self-esteem is primarily a matter of mind set,
of attitude—that you can psych yourself into peace of mind.
Peace of mind comes when your life is in harmony with true principles
and values and in no other way."
— Stephen Covey

"Again and again I therefore admonish my students in Europe and
America: Don't aim at success—the more you aim at it and
make it a target, the more you are going to miss it.

For success, like happiness, cannot be pursued; it must ensue,
and it only does so as the unintended side effect of one's personal
dedication to a cause greater than oneself or as the
by-product of one's surrender to a person other than oneself.

Happiness must happen, and the same holds for success:
you have to let it happen by not caring about it.
I want you to listen to what your conscience commands you to do
and go on to carry it out to the best of your knowledge.
Then you will live to see that in the long-run—
in the long-run, I say!—success will follow you
precisely because you had forgotten to think about it."
— Viktor Frankl

AN INTRO

Time for a quick intro to the key
themes of this little book. In short:
There are no secrets.
Integrity = Bliss.

A LOVER OF WISDOM

Alright. My hunch is you might be wondering who I think I am calling myself a "Philosopher." So, let's address that real quick-like, shall we?

First, a little language lesson.

The Classic Greeks had three words for love: *eros* (for sexual love), *agape* (for selfless love) and *philo* (for a brotherly sort of love).

Philo shows up in *philanthropist* (lover of people) and in one of my favorite words: *Philosopher* (*Philo* + *Sophia* = "lover of wisdom" where wisdom is knowledge of life).

Therefore, a Philosopher is, quite simply, someone in *love* with understanding how to create an authentically awesome life.

(Isn't that hot? I thought so, too.)

So, that's why I call myself a Philosopher. I'm super passionate about understanding how to live an extraordinary life as I make my little dent in the Universe.

How 'bout you?

THERE ARE NO SECRETS

Let's kick this party off by getting really clear on something: Optimal Living is NOT about the latest tips and tricks to help you get rich/enlightened/whatever quick. And we're definitely not going to talk about any "Secrets" that'll manifest shiny toys at your command.

Fact is, all the wisdom we need is already out there (and within us). The only question is: Is now a good time to start living it?

In this book we're gonna have fun tapping into the mojo of everyone from old-school rock stars to the modern positive psychologists.

Guess what they all say?

They tell us that creating a life filled with true meaning, joy, love, appreciation, creativity, wisdom, kindness, generosity, hope, optimism, energy, enthusiasm and all that goodness is about VIRTUE and INTEGRITY. We've gotta diligently, patiently, persistently and (very importantly!) playfully embody our truths and rock our fundamentals so that what we *say* is important to us aligns with who we are and how we show up in the world.

THE INTEGRITY GAP

Guys like Socrates, Plato and Aristotle tell us that if we want happiness, we've gotta live with *Areté*—a word that directly translates as "virtue" or "excellence" but has a deeper meaning, something closer to "living at your highest potential moment to moment."

I like to look at it this way:

Let's draw a couple lines—one representing what we're *capable* of doing/being in any given moment and one representing what we *actually* do/who we are in that moment.

Like so:

—————————————— Capable

—————————————— Actual

Now, if there's a GAP between what we're capable of doing/being and what we actually do/who we are, guess what sneaks in? Depression/anxiety/ick.

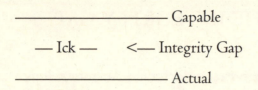

Often easier said than done, but close the integrity gap and there's no room for the negative stuff. Just a whole lot of happiness.

So, uh, how are *you* out of integrity and what can you start doing to close the gap?!

HAPPINESS = VIRTUES IN ACTION

Quick fact: In the 20th century, for every one hundred articles psychologists published on *negative* aspects of human behavior (stuff like depression, schizophrenia, etc.) there was only *one* article published on the positive stuff.

Basically, we figured out how to take someone from -10 to -5 to 0 through therapy and psycho-pharmacology, but we were pretty much in the dark on how to (scientifically) help someone go from 0 to +5 to +10 and beyond.

To address this issue, in the year 2000, Martin Seligman and Mihaly Csikszentmihalyi created a new movement called "Positive Psychology" that promised to identify the scientific underpinnings of how we can live with more happiness, meaning and all that good stuff.

Guess where they started.

They went Old School—sifting through all the classic wisdom texts where they saw the same ideas repeated again and again. Although they differ on the details, these classics (from the Bible to the *The Bhagavad Gita* to the

Bushido samurai code) say the same thing: Live with virtue.

In fact, the researchers identified a constellation of six core virtues: wisdom, courage, love, justice, temperance and spirituality. They set out to *scientifically* establish that, when we put these virtues in action, we'll live with more happiness, meaning and mojo.

The equation is simple: Happiness = Virtues in Action (VIA).

P.S. While we're on the subject of virtues in action, check out AuthenticHappiness.com and join a million other peeps who have taken their "VIA Character Strengths" test. It's an awesome way to identify your *scientifically* valid top virtues in action (aka strengths) so you can start engaging them more often in your day-to-day life.

As Martin Seligman, the author of *Authentic Happiness* and the Godfather of the Positive Psychology movement tells us, one of the keys to happiness is simple: Use your strengths often. Do so in service to something bigger than yourself and you'll be blessed with abundant happiness and a life filled with meaning and all that goodness to boot. Good times!

THE PRACTICE OF HAPPINESS

Thomas Jefferson declared that we all have the right to "Life, Liberty and the pursuit of Happiness."

That's a pretty powerful statement.

But, did you know that in Jefferson's day, the "pursuit of" something didn't mean you *chased* after it, it meant you PRACTICED it.[1] Like the pursuit of medicine. Or the pursuit of law. Or… the *pursuit of happiness.*

Happiness isn't some elusive treasure we chase after. It's a state of being we need to PRACTICE.

---

1 Picked this sweet idea up from Marci Shimoff's great book *Happy for No Reason.*

SPIRITUAL FARTS

Reverend Michael Beckwith[2] tells us that if we simply study and talk about spiritual truths but never actually LIVE the stuff, we're gonna get spiritual indigestion and constipation.

Spiritual farts.

It's not a pretty thing.

Seriously.

As the good Reverend and countless other teachers tell us, *theory* is *rudimentary* spirituality.

Practice? Actually LIVING it? That's the advanced stuff.

So, if you have some gas, please quit stinking up the room and start LIVING your truths, will ya?!

Thank you. Amen.

---

2 Michael Beckwith rocks. He created the transdenominational Agape International Spiritual Center in LA and wrote *Spiritual Liberation* (where I got this Idea). Check out the PhilosophersNote on the book for more goodness and if you're in LA and feelin' it, check him out. The man is plugged in!

YOUR #1s

Speaking of spiritual farts, if you're stinking up the room the easiest way to get everything back in order is by asking yourself two questions:

#1. What's the #1 thing I could *start* doing today that, if I did it consistently, would have THE most positive impact in my life? (Then do it.)

#2. What's the #1 thing I could *stop* doing right now, that, if I stopped doing it, would have the greatest positive impact in my life? (Then quit doing it.)[3]

Seriously, though. Whenever I find myself a little stressed/overwhelmed/whatever I ask myself these two questions—it's a REALLY powerful way to get the mojo back!

---

3 Shout out to Brian Tracy for first introducing me to these questions. Check out the PhilosophersNote on *Focal Point* and learn more about Brian at http://www.BrianTracy.com.

BLING TREADMILL

Researchers tell us that, at most, 10% of our happiness comes from stuff like fast cars, big houses, initials after our names or fancy titles on our business cards.[4]

Unfortunately, we've been conditioned to believe otherwise and most of us spend our lives chasing one thing after another—the bigger bank balance, the shinier bling, the higher altitude on the org chart—in our attempts to *finally* live with more happiness, peace, fulfillment and all that jazz. Psychologists call that being stuck on a "hedonic treadmill." Gasping and working but Never. Quite. Getting. There.

There's a much more direct way to sustainable happiness that comes from effectively shaping our thoughts and behaviors, living with virtue and being in integrity with our highest values.

Ultimately, we need to realize that the pursuit of all that fame/fortune/power is a lot like running in place.

So, let's step off the Bling Treadmill and diligently, patiently, persistently and playfully start focusing on what *really* matters—mastery of our thoughts and behaviors.

(Interestingly, the more we do this, the more the "material stuff" tends to show up—but more as by-products of our goodness than anything else!)

---

4 Check out Sonja Lyubomirsky's *How of Happiness* where she talks about the 50% of our happiness set points that come from our genetics, the 10% that come from life situations and the 40% that's under our direct control: our thoughts and behaviors.

THE 10 PRINCIPLES OF
OPTIMAL LIVING

From what I can see, the essence of Optimal Living comes down to these 10 Principles:[5]

1. **Optimism.** If we can't tame that crazy, drunk monkey in our mind and shape the contents of our consciousness, nothing else matters. Period.

2. **Purpose.** What inspires you? What's your dharma? Your purpose? Your highest calling? Living an authentically awesome life requires creating an empowering vision and keeping your eye on your Highest Goal without losing yourself on a manic Holy Grail chase.

3. **Self-Awareness.** From the Oracle of Delphi and the Buddha to modern science, it's clear: We've gotta know ourselves. How well do *you* know thyself?

4. **Goals.** Whether it's meditating first thing tomorrow morning or starting your business (or family or painting or...), we've gotta have goals that inspire us.

5. **Action.** All that's nice, but we've gotta follow Guru Nike's advice and *Just Do It!* Are you just doing it or just talking about it?

6. **Energy.** We're gonna have a hard time reaching our potential if we have a hard time getting out of bed or getting out of debt. Are you honoring the simple fundamentals of nutrition/exercise/rejuvenation/money?

7. **Wisdom.** Wisdom is all about approaching life as our classroom and looking at every moment as another opportunity to live our ideals.

8. **Courage.** The word comes from the Latin word for "heart." It's the virtue that pumps blood to all the other virtues. Without it, none of this other stuff matters. How's your courage pumping?

9. **Love.** Love, love, love. How're your relationships? Are you studying love like you'd study a sport or a musical instrument or a language you want to master?

10. **en*theos.** God/Spirit/The Universe. Whatever you call the Force that beats our hearts and keeps the planets in line, it's the center and circumference of everything. Connecting to it is a good idea. You plugged in?

---

5 This little book is organized around these principles. If you're feelin' it, check out http://www.OptimalLiving101.com for a 10-week class where I go into detail on all of 'em!

"Your mind will be like its habitual thoughts; for the soul becomes dyed with the color of its thoughts. Soak it then in such trains of thoughts as, for example: Where life is possible at all, a right life is possible."
— Marcus Aurelius

"Our life is shaped by our mind; we become what we think."
— Buddha

"The Master said, If out of the three hundred songs I had to take one phrase to cover all my teachings, I would say 'Let there be no evil in your thoughts.'"
— Confucius

"Everything can be taken from a man but one thing; the last of the human freedoms——to choose one's attitude in any given set of circumstances, to choose one's own way."
— Viktor Frankl

"All that is required to become an optimist is to have the goal and to practice it. The more you rehearse optimistic thoughts, the more 'natural' and 'ingrained' they will become. With time they will be part of you, and you will have made yourself into an altogether different person."
— Sonja Lyubomirsky

"A person can make himself happy, or miserable, regardless of what is actually happening 'outside,' just by changing the contents of consciousness. We all know individuals who can transform hopeless situations into challenges to be overcome, just through the force of their personalities. This ability to persevere despite obstacles and setbacks is the quality people most admire in others, and justly so; it is probably the most important trait not only for succeeding in life, but for enjoying it as well. To develop this trait, one must find ways to order consciousness so as to be in control of feelings and thoughts. It is best not to expect shortcuts will do the trick."
— Mihaly Csikszentmihalyi

OPTIMISM

It all starts with Optimism. If we can't tame those gremlins in our minds and learn to shape the contents of our consciousness, the rest of this stuff doesn't matter.

HELPLESSNESS & OPTIMISM

Optimism. It's Principle #1. All the great teachers—from Aurelius and the Buddha to the modern gurus and scientists—tell us the same thing: If we can't control the contents of our consciousness and tame those gremlins of fear and anxiety and self-doubt, none of the rest of this stuff matters. Period.

Before Martin Seligman started studying optimism and happiness and meaning, he spent a couple decades studying the opposite of optimism: helplessness.

Imagine a study with two dogs. They're both given shocks at random intervals. One can press a lever to stop the shocks. The other can't. The first dog quickly discovers how to stop the shocks and is fine. The other dog—the one who can't do anything about the shocks— eventually gives up and curls into a helpless little ball in the corner as the shocks continue. Eek.

That's Part I of the study.

Part 2: Those same dogs are put into a new environment. This time, both dogs can easily avoid the shocks. The healthy dog quickly discovers the trick and is fine. The other dog, EVEN THOUGH IT NOW HAS

THE POWER TO CHANGE THINGS, just gives up—curling into a ball as the shocks continue (and continue and continue). The dog has learned helplessness.

So have we.

After being shocked by life so many times throughout our lives, too often we "learn helplessness" and just give up—forgetting that, even though we might've been morons many times before, we ALWAYS (!!!) have the ability to choose a more effective response to whatever challenges we're currently facing.

KNOW THIS: Choosing to curl up in the corner (or in bed) as we helplessly let life shock us again and again is THE quickest way to ensure we're depressed (and, in the process, destroy our psychological and immunological health).

The antidote?

We've gotta learn optimism. Let's learn how. (But first, how about a look at crazy monkeys and ANTs?)

CRAZY LITTLE DRUNK
MONKEYS & ANTS

In Buddhism, they like to say that our minds are like monkeys swinging from thought to thought to thought. Only, the monkey in our mind is drunk, swinging from thought to thought to thought. Then, our little drunk monkey is stung by a scorpion! D'oh.

That's not all, though. Take that drunk little poisoned monkey and make him *crazy*!

THAT is how our minds tend to be.

Psychologists actually have a way to describe this as well. Apparently somebody figured out how to count all those monkey-swings and came up with the stat that we have, on average, about 60,000 thoughts per day. (Wow.)

Get this: 95% of *those* are *the same* thoughts from day to day to day. (Yikes.) AND, 80% of *those* thoughts are *negative*! (Yowsers!!!)

Daniel Amen calls them "automatic negative thoughts." ANTs for short. Whether we see our minds as filled with crazy little drunk monkeys or equally crazy little drunk ANTs, let's tame and sober 'em up!

OPTIMISM GYM

Let's say we're currently pretty pissy and pessimistic. Can we learn to be optimistic? Absolutely.

Martin Seligman wrote an entire book called *Learned Optimism*[6] where he outlines his suggested ways to get our optimism on (see "The 3 Ps of Optimism") and all the Ideas in this section are, essentially, about helping you build your optimism muscles.

Here's one way to think about it: A pessimist is the emotional equivalent of a couch potato whose idea of exercise is picking up the remote and taking a quick bathroom break during commercials. Totally flabby and out of shape and unhealthy.

If that pessimist wants to become a rock star triathlete-esque Optimist, he's gonna need to train. Hard. And not once in a while or when he *feels* like it but con-sistently. It's pretty much the *exact* same thing with our emotional well-being. We've gotta hit the Optimism Gym. Good news is membership's free. We just need to show up and do the work.

---

6 Awesome book. Check out the PhilosophersNote on it for my favorite goodness.

THE 3 PS OF OPTIMISM

From Martin Seligman's perspective, optimism is *not* about whistling happy tunes to ourselves when life gets challenging. It's about disciplining our minds to create more empowering explanations of what's going on.

Whether we're optimists or pessimists comes down to what he calls our "explanatory styles"—how we explain what's happening in our world. Specifically, in this model, it comes down to three Ps: Permanence, Pervasiveness and Personalization.

Imagine something good happens at work—let's say you get a promotion or land a big client or whatever qualifies as positive in your work world. How would you explain it?

Let's look at it through the 3 Ps. If you're a pessimist, you think the good fortune won't last (Permanence), it doesn't apply to the rest of your life (Pervasiveness) and it's because you got lucky (Personalization). If you're an optimist, you'll tend to see it the other way around: the good fortune will probably last, it's just another example of how everything's awesome in your life and it's probably the result of all the diligent, patient, persistent and playful hard work you've put in for quite a while.

Interesting, eh? Now, let's look at a negative event— let's say you are laid off or lose a big client or whatever. How do you explain it to yourself?

The pessimist, although convinced the positive stuff won't last, thinks the negative will last forever. And, although the positive event wasn't pervasive, the negative event is. And, although you wouldn't take any credit for the positive event, the negative event is totally your fault. D'oh.

On the other hand, the optimist looks at the negative event and believes it's just a temporary set-back (Permanence), is just one part of your life that's not as great as it could be (Pervasiveness) and is partly due to a poor economy so no need to take it all Personally.

Explanatory styles. Powerful stuff.

Check in on the good and "bad" stuff in your life. How are you interpreting them? Do you tend to have an optimistic or a pessimistic explanatory style?

The exciting news is that mastering our explanatory styles (like anything else) just takes practice. Next time you feel yourself swept away by a negative event or not fully appreciating a positive one, see if you can fine tune your Ps, please.

VICTIM VS. CREATOR

The difference between Optimism and Pessimism is really quite simple. It's all about *our orientation to the world.*

In any given moment we either choose (yes, it's a CHOICE) an empowering perspective or a disempowering one. We choose to be Victims or we choose to be Creators. The trick is to practice noticing when we're slipping into the Victim perspective.

So how do we catch ourselves?

If you're complaining, criticizing, blaming, gossiping and comparing, you can be pretty sure you're hanging out in Victimland—the unhappiest place on Earth.

Find the exit by asking yourself a simple question: *"What do I want?"*

Whereas the Victim constantly focuses on all the things that're *wrong* in their lives (and with everyone else around them—which is really just a reflection of all their inner angst), the Creator gets clear on what she wants.[7]

So, what do *you* want?

---

7 Check out the wise little fable called *The Power of TED** by David Emerald for more goodness on this!

RESPONSE-ABILITY

You can boil this whole optimism dealio down to one Idea: Are you response-able?

Can you step between stimulus and response and CHOOSE the most empowered response (or at least a much less crappy one)?

... Well, *can* you?

Pay attention the next time you feel yourself being triggered and see if you can sneak into that little space between stimulus and response and actually STOP the automatic/knee-jerk response and choose a more empowered one, yo!!

THE EQUANIMITY GAME

Marcus Aurelius,[8] the 2nd-century Roman emperor and Stoic Philosopher (who you might know from his cameo in the beginning of *The Gladiator*) tells us: *"When force of circumstance upsets your equanimity, lose no time in recovering your self-control, and do not remain out of tune longer than you can help. Habitual recurrence to the harmony will increase your mastery of it."*

That's strong.

Translation: When you find yourself off balance and life has kicked you in the butt, see how fast you can get back in balance. The more you practice this, the better you'll get.

---

8 Marcus Aurelius is one of my heroes. *Highly* recommend his *Meditations*—which is basically a collection of bite-size nuggets of wisdom from the journals he kept, reminding himself of the Stoic ideals to which he was committed.

THOUGHT TOOLS

Did you know the Sanskrit word *mantra* literally means "a tool of thought"?[9]

Yep. For thousands of years, people have reshaped their minds via the power of mantras. In addition to the cognitive behavioral stuff I go off on throughout this book, mantras are a great way to tame the monkeys and relocate the ANTs.

Our minds, as we learned, have a tendency to automatically generate negative thoughts—to the shocking range of 45,000 such negative little boogers a day. Mantras help us rewire our brains so, rather than automatic *negative* thoughts, we can get some automatic *positive* thoughts. ("APTs"—not quite as cute as ANTs but a heck-of-a-lot more enjoyable.)

The basic idea is simple. Reshape your mind through the repetition of certain phrases you find inspiring and empowering.

I've played with a *lot* of 'em at various times over the last decade.

Deepak has a few sweet ones I've said thousands of times that you might dig: *"I am totally independent of the good or bad opinion of others."* . . . *"I am beneath no one."* . . . *"I fearlessly approach any and all challenges in my life."*

My personal favorite might just be: *"Thank you, thank you, thank you, thank you, thank you!"* After repeating that I don't know how many times, I loved the day when my mind randomly whispered *"Thank you!"* to me in the middle of a quiet moment. (Pretty sweet APT, eh?! ;)

So, back to you: What are some of your favorite thought tools you can add to your Optimal Living tool belt?!

---

9 Shout out to vegan-yogi/hip-hop mogul Russell Simmons for the mojo on mantras from his great book *Do You!*

GOODNESS GARDENS

Let's say you want to create a beautiful garden. You pull the weeds, till the soil and plant and tend the seeds of the flowers you'd like to see one day bloom.

Nice.

If we want to create a beautiful life, we've gotta treat our minds and lives with the same care we would that garden—pulling out the weed thoughts/behaviors and only planting the seeds we want to see come to fruition.[10]

In other words, if you want a life filled with joy, love, appreciation, kindness, generosity, wisdom, patience, courage, creativity, and enthusiasm, PLANT THOSE SEEDS.

To think you're gonna get that goodness when you're constantly sowing the seeds of anger, fear, greed, impatience, laziness, half-assness, entitlement and whiny-ness just isn't very wise, eh?

So... What seeds are *you* planting, o' gardener?

---

10 This metaphor is common throughout the self-dev literature. Two of my favorite sources: Robin Sharma's *The Monk Who Sold His Ferrari* (fun novel all about creating an extraordinary life) and Pema Chödrön's *The Places That Scare You* (great Buddhist wisdom). PhilosophersNotes on both.

CONCRETE GARDENS

Pema Chödrön (a rockin' Buddhist nun) tells us we need to catch ourselves the moment we fall into old, negative patterns. Failing to do so is like pouring concrete over that (potentially) beautiful garden that is our lives.

And, well, concrete gardens pretty much suck. So, let's not do that.

Make it a game. See if you can catch yourself *right* as you slip into weenie-ville. Notice your pissiness, fear, anger, anxiety, overwhelm, RIGHT when it arises and see if you can aikido that energy into something more constructive. Doesn't matter what you do, just do ANYTHING other than the old destructive patterns.

Take a dozen deep breaths, go for a walk, sing a song, do a few pushups or jumping jacks, go for a run, whatever it takes to break the pattern and let your goodness garden bloom before you dump a ton of concrete all over it!

P.S. For the record, scientific research[11] supports this whole concrete garden dealio. Bad mood + rumination = toxic.

---

11 Check out Sonja Lyubomirsky's brilliant book, *The How of Happiness* (and/or my PhilosophersNote on it) for more goodness on that subject!

THOUGHT & BEHAVIOR POISONING

Eckhart Tolle tells us that, although it's important to accept ourselves and our emotions, it's also (really!) important to notice what behaviors and thoughts consistently lead to suffering and to QUIT DOING THOSE THINGS and to QUIT THINKING THOSE THOUGHTS!

He says it's kinda like getting food poisoning from eating certain types of food but then, for some wacky reason, you continue to eat those foods. And, as a result, you're sick again and again and again.

Makes *no* sense.

So, check yourself out and see if you're giving yourself thought and behavior poisoning on a regular basis.

And quit doing that.

LOVING WHAT IS

Byron Katie tells us that whenever she argues with reality she loses. But only every time.[12]

Love that.

Arguing with reality is a really silly idea. What's happened has happened and no amount of complaining on our part is going to change it.

So, while we may want to create a brighter future, the first step is (always) acceptance.

For the record, this acceptance is not some *"My life sucks and I accept my craptastic fate"* kinda thing. It's more like an *"Although this situation kinda blows, overall my life rocks and I'm going to accept what's happening and alchemize it into wisdom fuel as I continue to create my ideal life"* kinda thing.

---

12 Check out Byron Katie's awesome *Loving What Is* for some solid goodness on what she calls "The Work"—an inquiry process to help deal with reality more effectively. PhilosophersNote available as well.

ACCEPTANCE & SCRIPTING

How about some more goodness on acceptance plus another Tolle gem?

Sir Eckhart tells us that, when faced with a situation we can do *nothing* to change, rather than moan and wail and otherwise suffer, it makes a whole lot more sense to not only *accept* it, but to act as if you *scripted* the event to occur in your life.

That's a remarkably powerful way to go from Victim to Creator.

Fact is, as the great teachers tell us, every situation is essentially neutral/empty of meaning and we *always* have the power to choose THE most empowering interpretation of that event—or, of course, the least empowering interpretation.

Those moment-to-moment choices essentially determine whether we go through life joyfully or miserably.

So, choose wisely.

And, the next time you're faced with a train wreck, why not see if you can shift your perspective from *"OMG!*

Why did this happen to me?!" to *"What a fascinating event I scripted into my life. I wonder how I'm going to grow from this and how it can serve my Highest Goal of more consistently connecting to and expressing the Divine within me?!"*

I repeat: How we interpret an event is *always* within our control. Let's have fun choosing wisely!!

MASERATIS & BLIND DOODS

*D*ukkha. It's the word Buddhists use to describe the suffering inherent to life and comes from the ancient Pali word that describes a potter's wheel that isn't... quite... spinning... right. The axle's a little off and it screeches as it turns. Eek.

That's basically what happens to us way too often— we get stuck on a thought or in a certain perspective and can't... quite... let it... go.

Dukkha. It's that "stuckness" that creates our suffering. The essence of the Buddha's teachings is how we can get unstuck and experience the freedom of a mind that moves freely.

How about a couple Buddhist stories to help bring the point home?

First, Zen Master Genpo Roshi tells us to imagine we're driving a sweet Maserati.[13] And it's stuck in first gear. D'oh.

We may be stuck in first and not able to get out of bed in the morning or stuck in reverse and unable to drop something from the past or maybe we're stuck in fifth and can't slow down. In any case, if we can't easily shift gears, we're going to suffer. *Dukkha.*

Next: Load up six blind doods in that Maserati and drive 'em to a zoo where they can all experience an elephant for the first time.

The first guy touches the tail and is certain that an elephant is like a rope. The second guy touches the leg and is sure the elephant is like a pillar while the third guy goes for the tusk and says the elephant is like a spear. The other three go for different parts and have different perspectives (the back is like a throne; the trunk is like a tree branch; the ear is like a hand fan).

Now, what's fascinating is that they're all 100% certain *their* perspective is the *only* possible reality. *Dukkha.* (Anything like that ever happen to *you?*)

The lesson: We need to slide into *sukkha* by noticing when we think *our* perspective is the only one possible as we train ourselves to see multiple perspectives.

In short, next time you're stuck, remember to shift gears and to see the whole elephant. (How? Try to see the other person's perspective!)

---

13 Check out *Big Mind Big Heart* for all kinds of Zen goodness plus my PhilosophersNote on it for my favorite gems!

SIZES: YOU VS. YOUR PROBLEMS

Let's say, on a scale of 1-10, you're a size 1 or 2 person. You stub your toe in the morning or someone cuts you off on your way to work (size 1 problems). How do you respond?

You'll prolly get all pissy, eh? (For the record, if you're the kind of person who honks and yells and gets all road-ragey, you're about a .28.)

Now, let's say you're a size 8 or 9 person. Same stubbed toe and same person cutting you off. How do you respond?

You might just wince, take a deep breath, appreciate the fact that you're alive and your biggest problem at the moment is a stubbed toe. And, you might even bless that person who's in such a rush and wish them a safe trip and a more peaceful day.

Keep that in mind the next time you yell at someone on the freeway or otherwise get upset by something so trivial.

No need for us to be such small people in these precious lives of ours, eh?[14]

P.S. The way to go from 1 to 10? Simple. Live your values. Moment to moment, little by little, become more in integrity—so that what you *say* is important to you is what you actually do. Integrity. It's organic fertilizer for your character.

14 The idea of looking at the size of your problems vis-à-vis the size of your character is from T. Harv Eker's *Secrets of the Millionaire Mind!*

"Musicians must make music, artists must paint, poets must write if they are to be ultimately at peace with themselves. What human beings can be, they must be. They must be true to their own nature. This need we may call self-actualization... It refers to man's desire for self-fulfillment, namely to the tendency for him to become actually in what he is potentially: to become everything one is capable of becoming."
— Abraham Maslow

"Everything—a horse, a vine—is created for some duty... For what task, then, were you yourself created? A man's true delight is to do the things he was made for."
— Marcus Aurelius

"The Three Armies can be deprived of their commanding officer, but even a common man cannot be deprived of his purpose."
— Confucius

"It is better to strive in one's own dharma than to succeed in the dharma of another. Nothing is ever lost in following one's own dharma. But competition in another's dharma breeds fear and insecurity."
— Krishna

"Where there is no vision, the people perish."
— Proverbs 29:18

"This above all: to thine own self be true, and it must follow, as the night of the day, thou canst not then be false to any man."
— William Shakespeare

PURPOSE
& SELF-AWARENESS

What inspires you?
What's your dharma? Your
purpose? Your highest calling?
Living an authentically awesome
life requires knowing thyself +
an empowering vision.

HIGHEST GOALS
& HOLY GRAILS

Before we jump into this whole Purpose thing, let's get really clear on something. When I talk about discovering and living our purpose, I'm not talking about pausing everything in our lives and going out on a Holy Grail chase to discover something mysterious that's hidden somewhere hard to reach that only the lucky few ever discover.

Um, not so much.

Now, I definitely believe we all have a unique constellation of strengths and experiences and passions that blend together in ineffable ways, leading us to our most authentically awesome lives. But it's really easy to get all wrapped up in that and miss the fact that living a life of purpose isn't a *"someday when I've figured it all out and I've discovered my purpose I'll be happy and until then my life sucks"* kinda thing.

Nope.

Living a life of purpose is all about knowing that our Ultimate Purpose—our Highest Goal—is seeing just how consistently we can plug into the best within us.

In short, to live with integrity. (Yes, I'm repeating myself. It's deliberate. ;)

With THAT as our Ultimate Purpose and Highest Goal, EVERY MOMENT gives us an opportunity to be on purpose. And, well, that's awesome.

Plus, as it turns out, when we focus on our Highest Goal, we tend to be a *lot* happier *now* AND the specific purpose/dharma/destiny we're here to fulfill tends to come to us without so much fuss.

So, as we go out and rock it, let's remember the Ultimate Purpose Formula: Integrity = Bliss.

WRITE YOUR OWN STORY

Did you know the word "author" comes from the same root as the word "authentic"? Yeppers. To be authentic is to be the author of our own lives.

So, uh, who's writing *your* story?

SOUL OXYGEN

Abraham Maslow, the Great-Grandaddy in my spiritual family tree and 20th-century humanistic psychologist who studied the greatest people of his generation (including rock stars like Eleanor Roosevelt and Einstein) tells us that what one *can* be, one MUST be.

As we ascend his hierarchy of needs, taking care of the basics like food/shelter/safety and moving up through love and self-esteem we reach a place where we literally have a *need* to fully express ourselves—to, in Maslow's words "self-actualize."

Of course, it will take different forms for different peeps. But whether it's a calling to be an exceptional parent or artist or entrepreneur, Maslow tells us that this impulse isn't a sure-would-be-nice-to-have-fulfilled kinda thing but a fundamental NEED—kinda like that need we have for oxygen.

Powerful stuff.

So, the next time you're feeling funky, check in and see if you're really living fully or if you're only kinda-sorta showing up.

That funkiness is your soul gasping for the oxygen of you truly rockin' it.

P.S. Maslow sternly advises us: *"If you deliberately plan on being less than you are capable of being, then I warn you that you'll be unhappy for the rest of your life."* Eek.

All good though. He also reminds us: *"It seems that the necessary thing to do is not to fear mistakes, to plunge in, to do the best that one can, hoping to learn enough from blunders to correct them eventually."*[15]

P.P.S. So, plunge in!

---

15 Those two magical quotes are from Maslow's somewhat text-bookish (and expensive) but AMAZING *Motivation & Personality*. Good stuff. And, check out the PhilosophersNote for more on the 19 characteristics of the self-actualizer.

DEEPAK & DHARMA

Deepak's *The Seven Spiritual Laws of Success* wins my award for most-densely-packed-with-wisdom book out there. Reading the chapter on his 7th Spiritual Law (The Law of Dharma) literally changed my life a few years ago.

Basic idea: We all have a unique dharma/purpose/ destiny. It's our job in this little lifetime of ours to (1) connect to that higher force that beats our hearts and keeps the planets in line (best way to do that? meditation) as we (2) figure out what our unique gifts are and then (3) figure out how we're going to give those gifts in greatest service to our families/communities/world.

In the context of figuring out what our unique gifts are/what really inspires us (usually tied to one another, eh?), Deepak asks a question that literally left me stunned. It was this: *"If you had all the time and all the money in the world, what would you do?"*

I tend to take questions like that seriously. When I pondered it a few years ago, I didn't have a crystal clear answer but I knew it wasn't what I was doing. As a result, within weeks I wound up selling the biz I was running which led to the decision to give myself a Ph.D. in Optimal Living which led to me typing these words.

Now, I'm not suggesting you need to drop everything and turn your life upside down tomorrow, but it's a powerful question. And, in my experience (and as so many of the great teachers advise us), as we have the courage (and audacity) to really step into the possibilities of our lives (while working diligently, patiently, persistently, and playfully), amazing things open up for us. (And, of course, we also get our fair share of *"WTF did I do *that* for?!"* moments. :)

So, back to you: *"If you had all the time and all the money in the world, what would you do?"*

P.S. Here's another awesome question to help you find your Job with a capital J (as Jon Kabat-Zinn likes to call it): What do you love so much you'd *pay* to do it?

(I love learning and sharing and having great conversations with inspired peeps and feel blessed to have created a way to get paid to do that on a full-time basis. You?)

THE ULTIMATE END

Stephen Covey's 2nd Habit of Highly Effective People (right after "Be Proactive" and before "Put First Things First") is to "Begin with the End in Mind."

Basic idea is really simple: Everything is created twice—once in your mind/biz plan/blueprint and then in reality.

Same thing goes with our lives. If we want to create a truly extraordinary life, it's a good idea to know what a truly extraordinary life would look like, eh? With that in mind, how about taking a quick peek at the ultimate end?

Imagine this: Walk into a funeral—it can be in a place of worship or another sacred spot or wherever you feel most comfie imaging the ceremony. Get a feel for who's there. Check in to the energy. And then realize it's *your* funeral.

Boom!

So... Who says what?

What do your loved ones have to say about you? Your friends? Your colleagues? That clerk at the grocery store you saw so often?

What do they all have to say about you and what would you *like* them to say about you? That you were kind and patient and loyal and generous and inspiring and present and other such goodness?

Awesome. Are you living in Integrity with those deepest values of yours NOW?

(P.S. No one's going to say, *"What I loved most about So&So was that s/he had the biggest house on the block and always had the newest/fastest car and wore the most amazing sunglasses and..."* So, how about we start to focus a little more on the stuff that matters?)

DA VINCI & 100 QUESTIONS

Michael Gelb tells us we can learn *"How to Think Like Leonardo da Vinci."*[16]

How? By mastering the seven key aspects of da Vinci's genius. It all starts with the first quality of a master: Curiosity.

Gelb's book is packed with great stuff to help us get our curiosity on, including what may just be *the* most powerful journal exercise I've ever done. Goes something like this:

Find yourself a quiet place where you can relax with your journal for a good 45-60 minutes of uninterrupted Know Thyself time.

When you're nice and comfie, bust open your journal and write down 100 questions on *anything* you find interesting. Could be anything from *"Why is the sky blue and why are my boogers green?"* to *"What is my purpose in life?"* Just write whatever flows.

If you're like me, you'll prolly find that the first dozen or two come relatively easily then you might hit a tough spot and want to give up. Don't. Keep on writing even if you repeat yourself and/or don't feel totally inspired. You'll hit another burst of inspiration. Keep at it till you get to 100!

Once you've written your 100 questions, look back over them and see if you notice any themes. You talk about your professional or creative pursuits a lot? Your health? Your family? Spirituality? What themes emerge for you? Notice them.

Identify the Top 10 questions you find most inspiring. Which questions *really* fire you up? Write those down in a new place.

Then *rank order* those Top 10 questions from 1-10, with 1 being the most inspiring question out of the whole 100!

Now the fun's begun. It's time to make your life an answer to/expression of those questions!

---

16 This book rocks and is easily one of the most transformative books I've read. Check out the PhilosophersNote on it for some of my favorite Big Ideas and my own top 10 questions!

10 POWER QUESTIONS

Right after that 100 Questions exercise (you did it, right?), Gelb tells us that, in addition to being incredibly and insatiably curious, da Vinci was also committed to deep contemplation. If we want to be like Leo, we've gotta get our contemplation on!

To support that end, Gelb suggests we meditate on one or more of his "power questions."

I took him up on the invitation—writing *"How can I get paid to do what I love?"* on a piece of paper and hanging it, via some dental floss, over my shower head as I took a nice, long, contemplative bath.

(In many ways, I can trace typing these words to that precise moment when I decided I wanted to be paid to study life, become a better human being and share what I'm learning!)

I've created my own list of power questions. Ponder/ journal on these if you feel so inspired:

1. How can you use your strengths in greatest service to yourself, your family, your community and the world?

2. How can you get paid to do what you love?

3. What 5 things are you most proud of? What 5 things *will you be* most proud of?

4. If you had all the time and all the money in the world, what would you do?

5. What's your ideal day look like? When do you get up? What do you do? With whom? For whom? Imagine it in vivid detail!

6. Who are your heroes? Why? How are you like them?

7. What would you do if you weren't afraid?

8. If you were guaranteed to succeed, what's the #1 thing you would do? What else?

9. What is it that you and only you can do for the world?

10. How can you live in more integrity with your ideals? What's the #1 thing you could start doing that would have *the* most positive impact in your life? What's the #1 thing you could *stop* doing that would have the most positive impact in your life?! Sweet. Now rock it.

HOW'S YOUR GENIUS?

Get this: Back in the Roman Empire's days of sexy togas and sweet sandals they believed *everyone* had their own little mini-Me-like Genius—a guiding spirit that helped 'em rock it.

If anyone did something amazing—whether it was artistic or athletic or rhetorical—it was said their "genius" had guided them.

How cool is *that*?!? (Correct answer: Very. :)

Good news: It's still true. We ALL have our own genius within. The question is: How's yours?

Elizabeth Gilbert (author of *Eat Pray Love*) did a super cool TED talk[17] where she points out the fact that, although it's her inner genius who's responsible for the creative goodness that might come through her on any given day, it's HER responsibility to show up to write.

Love that.

How 'bout you? What do you need to do to make sure your genius knows you wanna play?

---

17 Check it: http://www.ted.com/talks/elizabeth_gilbert_on_genius.html

110-YEAR-OLD YOU

Tal Ben-Shahar,[18] one of the world's leading Positive Psychologists and teacher of one of the most popular classes in Harvard University's history, tells us that we already have all the wisdom we need.

He points to individuals who have near-death experiences or life threatening illnesses who suddenly (and permanently) change their lives—creating meaning and happiness that hadn't been there before that moment.

Essentially, they always *knew* what to do, but they weren't actually doing it till life gave them a kick in the butt.

He has this BRILLIANT exercise to help us tap into the wisdom that's already percolating in our consciousness. It goes something like this: You're 110-years-old. NASA (or Richard Branson's Virgin Time Travel ;) just invented a time machine. It can take you back to THIS moment so your 110-year-old self has 30 minutes to chat with your current you.

What do you tell yourself?!? What are the most important truths/lessons/Big Ideas you'd want to share in that 30 minutes?

What if you only had 5 minutes? What would you share? What if you only had 60 seconds? What's THE most important message you'd want to share?!

Let's write that down. If my 110-year-old version of myself appeared in front of the current version of me *right now* this is what I'd tell myself:

_____

_____

_____

_____

_____

whispers

... Now's a (really) good time to start paying attention to that advice...

---

18 Check out Tal Ben-Shahar's great books, *Happier* (where he outlines some Big Ideas from the Positive Psych movement and the über-popular class he taught at Harvard and where I discovered this exercise), and *The Pursuit of Perfect* (where he gives sage advice to all of us perfectionists out there!). PhilosophersNotes on both.

*"When you want something, all the universe conspires
in helping you to achieve it."*
— Paulo Coelho

*"Avoid fragmentation: Find your focus and seek simplicity. Purposeful
living calls for elegant efficiency and economy of effort—expending the
minimum time and energy necessary to achieve desired goals."*
— Dan Millman

*"It turns out that the process of working toward a goal,
participating in a valued and challenging activity,
is as important to well-being as its attainment."*
— Sonja Lyubomirsky

*"Attaining lasting happiness requires that we enjoy the journey
on our way toward a destination we deem valuable.
Happiness is not about making it to the peak of the mountain
nor is it about climbing aimlessly around the mountain;
happiness is the experience of climbing toward the peak."*
— Tal Ben-Shahar

GOALS

Whether our goal is to live with
love/appreciation/joy/kindness/
generosity/and-all-that-goodness or
to start a business, compete in
a triathlon or create
financial freedom,
Goals are important.

BLING VS. BEING GOALS

Goals. They're super important. But, from my perspective, people spend *way* too much time setting bling goals when they should be focusing that energy on being goals.[19]

Two important reasons why the near exclusive focus on "having"/"stuff" goals is a bad idea:

1. As we've discussed, acquiring stuff doesn't lead to happiness. Changing your thoughts and behaviors does.

2. Outcomes are simply by-products of consistently rockin' it, so it makes a heck-of-a-lot more sense to set creative production goals and blissipline goals than it does to obsess about outcomes.

---

19 Examples of "being" goals: Being more kind, generous, optimistic, courageous, loving, etc. Basically, living with more virtue.

RUBBER BANDS & YOUR IDEALS

Grab a rubber band.

Stretch it between the pointer fingers of your left and right hands. (Pretty, please.)

Feel that tension?

Let's imagine that your left hand is your current reality and your right hand, stretching away from the left, is your ideal. That tension is called "dynamic tension."[20] It's a good thing.

But most people don't like that feeling. It's a little uncomfortable.

Way too often, we do everything we can to escape that dynamic tension. We quit dreaming and pull our ideals back. Or we manically chase after insane goals and then collapse. Or we numb ourselves with another beer or another glass of wine or another hour of TV or another hour online.

Those are *not* good things.

What we wanna do is be honest about (and love) where we're at, get giddy about our goals, and hold the tension as we (joyfully) take the next (baby) step in the direction of our dreams. And then the next step and the next step and the next step and the next—diligently, patiently, persistently and playfully.

And, sure enough, we're moving toward our ideal and our ideal is moving toward us. And life feels splenderrific. (That's the technical description. :)

So, how're you doing with your rubber bands and your ideals? Have a clear vision of your ideal? Loving (!) where you're at? Taking baby steps in the direction of your dreams?!

Let's get practical: What's your most important goal and what step can you take right now in its direction?

My #1 Goal: _____

My Next Baby Step: _____

(Now's always a good time for that next step, btw. ;)

---

20 This is another great Idea from David Emerald's *The Power of TED**. Bought 25 for Christmas presents one year. Highly recommend it!

COMFORT, STRETCH
& SNAP ZONES

Still have your rubber band? Sweet.

So, if we stay in our comfort zones all our lives, we aren't gonna feel too great. That's pretty straight-forward. (Imagine a limp rubber band. No stretching. Not so good.)

The challenge is, if we're constantly setting ridiculous goals we expect to hit in ridiculous time frames, we're not gonna feel too great either. (That would be the equivalent of pulling the rubber band so hard it snaps. Ouch.)

Raise your hand if you've been there and done that. (Both of my hands are currently up.)

The trick? We've gotta find the *stretch zone*[21] between our comfort zones and our snap zones—that place where we're stretching ourselves... but not so much we snap!

The problem is we want everything and we want it NOW. Um, yah. Let's chillax a bit, set some fun, authentically inspiring stretch goals and then diligently, patiently, persistently and playfully stretch ourselves, shall we?

---

21 Inspired by Tal Ben-Shahar and his awesome comfort-stretch-panic zone model from his equally awesome book, *Happier!* Check out the PhilosophersNote on it for some of my favorite goodness.

THE TOLLE TRAP

In addition to having the world's greatest sweater-vest collection, Eckhart Tolle has some really powerful ideas for optimal living. But I think a lot of people who get all horny about creating A New Earth via the Power of Now fall into what I call "The Tolle Trap"—where it's *ALL* about being in the moment. (D'oh. It's not.)

In his fab book, *Happier*, the good Dr. Tal Ben-Shahar articulates four different "archetypes" that provide a useful model to help us conceptualize (and address) the problem. Here's my take on it:

- **The Rat Racer:** The typical Western mode of being. Always chasing goals we're told matter, never really happy because we're Never. Quite. There.

- **The Hedonist:** The typical "spiritual" way of being. Misreading Tolle and the *Gita*, thinking it's ALL about *just* being in the moment. (Eek.)

- **The Nihilist:** Bounces back and forth between those two then flips everyone (and everything) off and becomes the cynic (aka, a disillusioned idealist).

- **The Happy Person:** Realizes life is all about having goals that inspire us AND loving this moment as we take baby steps in the direction of our ideals.

It's easy to bounce around all four ways of being, but let's not kid ourselves that we're either happy *or* spiritual as we pretend to "get it" and just love love love the power of now.

Fact is, even Tolle appreciates the importance of goals and provides some great advice on the subject—telling us goals are important but that we want to make sure we don't let what he calls "clock time" slip into "psychological time."

The difference?

Healthy human beings use clock time to set goals and organize their tasks accordingly.

Unhealthy human beings slip into psychological time as they waste energy getting anxious about the outcomes of future events or they get their panties/undies in a bunch with guilt/shame about past events. OR, they lose their vitality and overall life mojo as they fall into The Tolle Trap of trying to avoid goals altogether. (Or, they do all three. ;)

How about you? Where are *you* hanging out? How can you more consistently play in the happiness zone? Do you need more truly inspiring goals? More presence?

Let's set some goals that inspire us, love where we're at and have fun taking the next step in the direction of our dreams!

YOUR ANGEL'S ADVOCATE

We all know about the devil's advocate. But what about the "angel's advocate"?

From my vantage point, it sure looks like our angels are underemployed. Of course, it's important to prepare for what can go wrong, but what about spending more time looking at all the things that can go *right* in our lives?!

Me thinks it's time to put our angels to work.

Imagine your little angel taking its rightful place above your right shoulder. Is it a he or a she? Name? Tattoos/other distinguishing features? Got a good image?

Nice.

Now, like all good angels, your angel likes to work hard. So, ask that little guy/gal of yours: *"If everything went incredibly, splendidly right, what would my life look like?"*

Write it down. The more details the better!

And remember: Your angel loves to imagine all the things that can go right with a creative project or business or relationship or any and everything else in your life. So, put 'em to work, yo!

P.S. This isn't just another woo woo self-development exercise. Psychologists call exercises like this a "Best Selves Diary" and they've been scientifically proven to develop our optimism—which, as we now know, is a key variable to our overall well-being. So, give it a shot if you're feelin' it!

P.P.S. I start pretty much every creative project with a little angel's advocate journaling and love to do it if I'm ever feeling a bit stuck!

*"We fail to realize that mastery is not about perfection.
It's about a process, a journey. The master is the one who stays
on the path day after day, year after year. The master is the one who
is willing to try, and fail, and try again, for as long as he or she lives."*
— George Leonard

"Good thoughts are no better than good dreams, unless they be executed!"
— Ralph Waldo Emerson

*"Vision is not enough; it must be combined with venture.
It is not enough to stare up the steps; we must step up the stairs."*
— Vaclav Havel

*"You must be the kind of man who can get things done. But to get things
done, you must love the doing, not the secondary consequences."*
— Ayn Rand

*"The great French Marshall Lyautey once asked his gardener to plant
a tree. The gardener objected that the tree was slow growing and
would not reach maturity for 100 years. The Marshall replied,
'In that case, there is no time to lose; plant it this afternoon!'"*
— John F. Kennedy

"Try not. Do or do not. There is no try."
— Yoda

ACTION

As the Greek guru Nike tells us,
at some point it's time to
just do it, eh? Indeed it is.
Diligently, patiently, persistently
and playfully, of course.

FOLLOW YOUR BLISS
(& YOUR GRUNT)

"*Follow your bliss.*"

Gotta love that classic line from Joseph Campbell.

You know how he came up with it?

Among (many) other things, Campbell was a Sanskrit scholar and, as he was editing some stuff back in the day, he came across the Vedic notion that there are three jumping-off points into enlightenment: *sat* (being-ness), *chit* (consciousness), and *ananda* (bliss or rapture).

Campbell said that if he was honest with himself he didn't know what proper "being-ness" was, nor did he know what proper "consciousness" was. But his bliss? His rapture? THAT he could trust.

Enter: *"Follow your bliss!"*[22]

Of course, it's easy to get all geeked up about such an inspired idea and see it as a license to do whatever we want whenever we want which is why, later on in his life, Campbell once joked that he wished he had said, *"Follow your grunt!"*

As it turns out, there's actually a word for *that* in

Sanskrit as well. It's called *tapas*[23]—the idea that hard work and disciplined effort can burn away the impurities that keep up separate from the Divine. Powerful stuff.

So, I hereby preach: Follow your bliss!

And, equally importantly: Follow your grunt!

---

22 Picked that up from *The Power of Myth*—the great book that captures some of the wisdom that didn't make it into the Bill Moyers interviews by the same name (which, if you haven't watched yet, is a must!).

---

23 Shout out to Russell Simmons, the coolest (and only?) vegan hip-hop mogul yogi out there who introduced me to this idea in his great book *Do You!*

BLISSIPLINE

Discipline. It's the secret sauce.

In a world where we want everything RIGHT. THIS. SECOND. we seem to have forgotten (or just *really* like to ignore) the fact that *nothing* of any value comes without a whole heck-of-a-lotta work.

S.N. Goenka,[24] the Vipassana meditation teacher whose organization led the 10-day silent meditation ~~boot-camp~~ course I attended a few years ago said this dozens (and dozens) of times throughout the training:

—> Quick FYI: For the full effect, you've gotta imagine him saying this in a slow, hypnotic, lyrical Burmese-accented voice! <—

"Work diligently. Diligently. Work patiently and persistently. Patiently and persistently. And, you're bound be successful. Bound to be successful."

Think about it.

If we actually work diligently, patiently, and persistently we ARE BOUND to be successful. Now, the success may or may not be in the exact form or on the precise timeline we imagined, but we most certainly will be successful.

That's hot.

I'm into enjoying the whole process so I like to throw in "playfully."

Work *diligently, patiently, persistently* and *playfully* and we're not only *bound to be successful,* we're bound to have a great time and feel really (!) good throughout this whole experience called life.

And, our discipline turns to blissipline[25] as doing what's best for us is what we most enjoy doing![26]

---

24 Vipassana is a Buddhist mindfulness meditation practice and the 10 days of silence/10 hours of meditation a day was not only one of the most challenging things I've done, but the most transformative. I talk about some of my biggest lessons learned in my PhilosophersNote on James Allen's *As a Man Thinketh* and you can learn more about Vipassana meditation and sign up (if you dare!) here: http://www.dhamma.org

---

25 *Blissipline*. Isn't that word sexcellent?!? I got it from Michael Beckwith in his *awe-some* book, *Spiritual Liberation*. Check the book and my PhilosophersNote on it for more Blissipline goodness.

---

26 Seneca (in *Letters from a Stoic*) says it best: *"How much better to pursue a straight course and eventually reach that destination where the things that are pleasant and the things that are honorable finally become, for you, the same."*

CONSISTENCY ON THE FUNDAMENTALS

Robin Sharma studies greatness.[27] Guess what he says *all* great people have in common.

(If you looked at the title of this little chapter and guessed "Consistency on the fundamentals!" you win.)

Sharma tells us that although the specific manifestation of one's greatness may take the form of being an extraordinary athlete, political leader, entrepreneur, artist, musician, etc., what you'll find among all masters is a passionate consistency on their fundamentals. They show up day in and day out and rock the stuff that's most important to making them exceptional in their field.

Consistency on the fundamentals. Kinda synonymous with Blissiplines, eh? And kinda begs the question: What are YOUR fundamentals?

My current fundies? I meditate every day. I move every day. I study/reflect/journal every day. I appreciate (my wife and life) every day. I strive to give joy and enjoy every day.

Yours?

---

27 Check out Robin's *Greatness Guide*. Awesome booked packed with genius Big Ideas.

+I OR -I?

Abraham Maslow liked to say that in any given moment we have a choice: Will we step forward into growth or back into safety?

Moment by moment by moment, we make a choice. And we shape our destiny.

I like to think of it like this: It's almost as if we have a little subconscious computer that's keeping score for us. +I if we choose to step forward into growth, -I if we choose to step back into safety.

+I or -I. +I or -I. +I or -I.

Let's say the alarm goes off tomorrow morning. Do we step forward and do the thing we said we'd do—whether it's jumping out of bed and immediately meditating/going for a run/whatever?

OR, do we step back into safety and pull the covers over our head as we try to forget what we said we'd do and come up with some lame rationalization about how we need the rest, blah blah blah blah whiny blah?

+I or -I.

Alright. You kicked your day off with that decision.

Now, let's move through your day. Moment to moment to moment. Forward into growth or back into safety? Forward into growth or back into safety?

+1 or -1? +1 or -1? +1 or -1?

Now, fast-forward to the end of the day. You're either at +10,000 or -10,000 or, likely, somewhere in between. Pay attention because if you were out of integrity all day long, those negative numbers are gonna eat at your soul and are usually accompanied by a strong urge to snap at your wife/husband/kids and/or to numb yourself from the pain with another beer or glass of wine or hour of TV or web surfing or [insert you're favorite numbing activity here].

Do that day after day after day and, well, you're gonna either be seriously depressed or addicted to something (or both) or in some other state of dis-ease.

Good news though: A few strong positive steps forward can have a mysteriously magical effect. And we *always* have the choice to take that step forward.

So, what's a +1 step you can take right now?

(P.S. Now's a good time to take it. I'll be here when you get back. ;)

A PENNY FOR YOUR PERSISTENCE

You might've heard of the old power-of-compounding-interest story from your friendly CPA advising you to invest in your 401k. It's a great metaphor for improving your life a little every day.

Two options for you: I'll give you $2.5 million today or I'll give you a penny today and double that penny every day for a month. Which one would you like?

Insert Jeopardy music here

So… Which one did you pick?

And, before you answer, are you curious which month it is? Because if it's February, you'd be better off with the $2.5 million now but if it's any other month, you'd be ahead with the penny doubling.

On Day 28 that magical doubling penny is worth $1,342,177.28.

On Day 31 it's worth $10,737,418.24.

Amazing what those last few days do for us, eh?

Back to the life application: Quit going for the secret trick that'll magically make you a happy rock star. Go for the slow but steady day-by-day improvements and, OVER THE LONG RUN, you'll be way ahead.

P.S. Here's an awesome question to help you count your pennies: At the end of every day ask yourself, *"Self* (Note: It's VERY important you refer to yourself as "Self" ;), *did we get a little better today?"*

String a decade full of "Yayuh!"s together and you're sittin' pretty.

BLISTERS & BLISS

John Wooden was arguably *the* greatest coach of all time in any sport. The guy won 10 championships in 12 years at UCLA and had an 88-game undefeated streak that ran nearly 3 years. (Go Bruins! :)

Wooden was all about consistency on the fundamentals and had an awesome way of kicking off each season. Imagine the greatest young basketball players in the US showing up for the first day of practice. Guess what Coach would start with...

He'd show them how to put on their socks.

Why? Because if they couldn't put their socks on just right, they might get a blister. Get a blister and they might miss practice time. Miss practice time and their game-time performance would suffer.

The equation was simple: Blister = No championship.

Amazing.

Kinda begs the question: Any "blisters" slowing you down?

If so, you might wanna look at how you're putting on your socks.

Fact is, when we don't pay attention to the little things, we're gonna get blisters. Tragically, rather than see that our blisters (aka depression/anxiety/fatigue) are caused by the wrinkles in our socks (lack of exercise/lack of inspiring goals/lack of commitment/whatever other fundamentals we're ignoring), we reach for the nearest band-aid (antidepressant/remote control/beer) and *totally* ignore the CAUSE of our various blisters.

D'oh. Not a good idea. Makes a whole lot more sense to slow down a bit and get those socks on nice and neat, eh?

Identify your fundamentals. What are the things that, when you do them consistently, make you feel GREAT?!

It might be meditating daily, exercising, journaling, doing yoga, keeping a gratitude log, reading inspiring wisdom, pursuing goals that fire you up, choosing to see the positive in challenges (or all of the above!), but whatever your fundamentals are, you've gotta get REALLY clear on 'em and develop the blissipline to crush it. Yah?

99% IS A BITCH.
100% IS A BREEZE

Jack (*Chicken Soup for the Soul*) Canfield has a great line. He says: *"99% is a bitch. 100% is a breeze."*

Classic.

Are you looking to start a new habit? That thing you just *know* you could be doing that'd totally take your life to the next level if you did it consistently? Might be meditating, exercising, journaling, reading more, eating well or some other empowering habit you could add to your life.

Or, you might be trying to *stop* an old habit— might be no longer yelling at your kids or zoning out in front of the TV, aimlessly surfing the Internet, smoking, drinking, whatever.

If you've failed to make a habit either stick or go away, I'd be willing to bet you have a 99% (at best) commitment.

But, as Sir Canfield tells us, 99% is a bitch. 100%? That's where it's at.

Let's say you commit to meditating every day for the rest of your life (one of my commitments that I've been rockin' for two+ years at this point). You're BOUND to wake up one day with that whiny little voice inside your head that says: *"You know, we deserve a day off today. I mean, come on. We're tired. What's ONE day off? Don't be a freak about it. Relax."*

If you only have a 99% commitment you might respond with: *"Hmmm... You know, you're right. We *do* deserve a day off, huh? One day won't hurt. Yah, let's take today off then we'll crush it tomorrow."*

And, wham. You're screwed. Habit installation thwarted. Ten days later you wonder what happened to your meditation practice.

The solution? We've gotta identify what's REALLY (!) important in our lives. Then pick ONE thing we're absolutely, 100% committed to rockin' and make our commitment NON-NEGOTIABLE.

Not 99% or 99.8%. 100%.

Then, when that little whiney voice pops up (which it will), we just ignore it and go on with creating an awesome life. (So, uh, what are you gonna make a 100% commitment to?)

LITTLE BY LITTLE

The Buddha tells us that one becomes good little by little—as a water pot is filled with water, drop by drop by drop. (He also tells us that one becomes evil, little by little, drop by drop by little decision drop.)

Little by little. Drop by drop.

Little by little. Drop by drop.

After years of trying to fill my water pot ALL! AT! ONCE!, I'm finally understanding that my attempts to change everything NOW were like trying to fill a beautiful, delicate water pot with a fire hydrant. Rather than winding up with a full pot, I pretty much sprayed the thing all around the room (and nearly cracked it!).

Little by little. Drop by drop.

That's the way to roll.

Moment by moment. Little decision by little mundane decision. Day in and day out. THAT's where it's at.

HIT THE ROCK

While we're learning how to fill a water pot, how about a little mojo on how to hit a rock?

Ever heard the story about the stonecutter?

Goes like this: A stonecutter hits a rock with his sledgehammer. The stone splits. The casual observer happens to walk by right at that moment and thinks: *"Wow. That guy is super strong. I can't believe he broke that huge rock with a single blow!"*

The reality (obviously) is that the stonecutter didn't break it in a single blow—he'd been hammering away at that rock for a long, long time. A lot of diligent effort went into that rock before it finally split.

That's kinda analogous to how people often respond to someone who's achieved a high level of success and think: *"Wow, they sure must be lucky."*

Obviously, the stonecutter isn't strong enough to break a rock in one blow and no one is "lucky" enough to reach any level of sustainable success without an equally diligent and consistent effort.

As Thomas Jefferson reminds us, the harder he worked,

the luckier he got. And Emerson tells us that good luck is just another name for tenacity of purpose.

So, let's hit the rock. Again. And again. And again. Eventually, it'll break.

(Oh, and btw: Once you're done with that rock get ready to start swinging at the next one. :)

NOW WHAT NEEDS
TO BE DONE?

Feeling depressed? Don't want to get out of bed? Sweet. *Now what needs to be done?*

Feeling overwhelmed and want to give up? Awesome. *Now what needs to be done?*

Feeling [insert your favorite crappy emotional state here] and want to [insert your favorite coping mechanism here]? Rockin'. *Now what needs to be done?*

Now what needs to be done?

Now what needs to be done?

Now what needs to be done?

That's the mantra of David Reynolds' *awesome* little book *Constructive Living*—which wins my award for "Best Book You've Probably Never Heard Of." (Genius recommendation from my friend Dan Millman.)

Somewhat random side note: I have a tattoo of the Sanskrit symbol for the third chakra on the inside of my right wrist that represents the power of self-mastery and reminds me to live impeccably. It's basically shorthand for: *"Now what needs to be done?"*

DO YOUR HABITS FIT?

Did you know the word *habit* originally referred to the clothes you wore? Yep.[28]

Your habits "fit" who you are.

So, how are YOUR ~~clothes~~ habits?

You rockin' the style you wanna be seen in or are you still wearing tattered, mis-fitting, hand-me-down habits from a less evolved version of you?!? Know that if you want to change your life, the fastest way is to change your habits.

With that in mind, I say it's time to clean out your closet and go shopping for some new habits!

Shopping spree: What are some new awesome habits you could develop in your life?

Closet cleanse: What are some old less-than-awesome habits that need to go?

---

28 Picked this one up from Maxwell Maltz's classic *Psycho-Cybernetics*. Check out my PhilosophersNote on it for more goodness.

JORDAN, MOZART
& 10,000 HOURS

Did you know Michael Jordan wasn't even the best athlete in his family as a kid? Nope. It wasn't until MJ didn't make the Varsity team his sophomore year in high school that he decided to turn it up about ten notches and become one of the hardest working athletes of his generation. And, as a result, one of the best.

People don't like to hear about that though. We prefer to think of Air Jordan as a born genius rather than an über-hard working guy who CREATED his genius. (Much easier to say the great ones were born lucky than to realize we might be capable of a whole lot more than we're up to, eh?)

How about Mozart? Born a genius, right?

Not if you scratch the surface of that myth. Mozart was born the son of Leopold Mozart, who just so happened to, *literally*, write the book on how to teach kids music. Fact is, Mozart watched his dad teach his sister music from the day he was born and was hard at work barely out of his diapers. Sure, he did extraordinarily precocious stuff as a little guy but we need to look at how *hard* he worked and how many hours of deliberate practice he'd put in by the time he created something truly world-class.

10,000 hours. If you believe the experts,[29] that's the magic number. 10,000 hours (or about 4 hours a day 5 days a week 50 weeks a year for 10 years!) of what they call "deliberate practice"—when we're at our edge, challenging ourselves to develop new skills in a given domain.

From violinists to programmers. Athletes to entrepreneurs. 10,000 hours of deliberate practice.

We may or may not want to invest the energy necessary to achieve greatness, but let's not pretend these peeps were "born" with the greatness gene.

And, for those of us who ARE committed to doing something great, how're your 10,000 hours?

---

29 Some of my favorite books on this that you might dig include *Outliers* by Malcolm Gladwell, *Talent Is Overrated* by Geoff Colvin and *The Talent Code* by Daniel Coyle. Great reads!

COMMITMENTS
& COMPLETIONS

Do you honor your commitments? You know, when you say you're going to do something, do you?

Or, do you tend to make a lot of commitments and then drop a lot of balls—letting yourself and others down in the process?

Getting in the habit of honoring our commitments is *huge.* Fact is, we simply can't function optimally when we're dropping commitments left and right.

To develop integrity, quit making so many commitments and *really* check in *before* you make your next commitment and confirm to yourself that you will, fer sure, follow thru.

And, you might want to take a quick inventory of your *current* commitments: Are there any you've been avoiding you can knock out pretty quickly? Maybe some require communication about a new commitment/new timeline? And, maybe you're no longer committed to some (or maybe never were) that you need to tell someone about?

Getting completions on our commitments is big. So, let's.

ONE TOUCHING

Here's a cool little "completions" tool: See how many things you can "one touch."

If you get an email that requires less than a couple minutes of effort, "one touch" it with a quick response. (And *definitely* delete it if you never need to look at it again. But, whatever you do (unless you really enjoy the inbox hell of hundreds of opened yet not resolved emails), DON'T leave stuff in there to pile up!)

Same with bills. One touch 'em—have fun walking in from the mailbox, opening the bills, writing the checks and walking back out to the mailbox. Done.

There's something magical about getting little things done efficiently.

(And, I really need to do this more. :)

RE-COMMITMENT

It's easy to commit to something—whether it's losing weight, no longer yelling at the kids (or spouse or colleagues or all of the above), creating that business, writing the screenplay, whatever.

It's an entirely different thing to actually *honor* that commitment—*especially* when you're all up in your stuff and you don't feel like it and that whiny little gremlin in your head has taken over the airwaves. (Hate when that happens.)

To actually rock it?

Step 1: Commitment.

Step 2: Re-commitment.[30]

Step 3: Re-commitment.

Step 4: Re-commitment.

Step 5: You get the idea.

How 'bout you? Need to re-commit to something?

---

30 Picked this one up at a Hendricks Institute workshop. http://www.hendricks.com

THE 80/20 PRINCIPLE

D id you know that 20% of beer drinkers drink 80% of the beer?

Yep.

And 20% of married people get 80% of the divorces? And 20% of roads have 80% of the traffic? And that you probably wear 20% of your clothes 80% of the time?

Yep. Yep. Yep.

And how 'bout the fact that 80% of the wealth of 20th-century England was in the hands of 20% of its noble class?

Yep. The good ol' Vilfredo Pareto, an Italian economist, discovered that last bit of data—which led to him articulating the phenomenon known as "The Pareto Principle" or, more commonly, "The 80/20 Principle."[31]

Why should you care?

Well, the fact is that (somewhere around) 20% of your activity is leading to (somewhere around) 80% of your results—whether we measure it as happiness/ profits/health/well-being/whatever.

(Which, for the non-mathematicians in the crowd, means we're wasting a *lot* of time/energy on stuff that just doesn't matter and that we just don't enjoy that much.)

So, it makes a *lot* of sense to identify those few things (and people!) that give us the most benefit/joy and (most importantly!) focus on 'em.

Unfortunately, most of us are "too busy" (ick) doing the stuff that doesn't really matter to slow down long enough to identify what *really* matters.

My vote?

Let's do an inventory of the 20% that gives us the most joy as we remember Goethe's wisdom: *"Things which matter most must never be at the mercy of things that matter least."*

---

31 Check out Richard Koch's brilliant book *The 80/20 Principle: The Secret to Success by Achieving More with Less* (and my PhilosophersNote on the book) for more 80/20 mojo!

"The best way to make a fire with two sticks is to make sure one of them is a match."
— Will Rogers

"The more I observed human behavior, the more convinced I became that the key to health is understanding each person's individual needs, rather than following a set of predetermined rules. I saw plenty of evidence that having happy relationships, a fulfilling career, an exercise routine and a spiritual practice are even more important to health than a daily diet."
— Joshua Rosenthal

"No one in our society needs to be told that exercise is good for us. Whether you are overweight or have a chronic illness or are a slim couch potato, you've probably heard or read this dictum countless times throughout your life. But has anyone told you—indeed, guaranteed you— that regular physical activity will make you happier? I swear by it."
— Sonja Lyubomirsky

"The goal should not be to make money or acquire things, but to achieve the consciousness through which the substance will flow forth when and as you need it."
— Eric Butterworth

"Meditation is warm-up exercise for the mind, so that you can jog through the rest of the day without getting agitated or spraining your patience."
— Eknath Easwaran

ENERGY

We're gonna have a hard time living at our highest potential if we have a hard time getting out of bed (or out of debt), eh? We've gotta create radiant mind/body/spirit health so we have the mojo to rock it!

GAS & SAWS

Are you too busy to take care of yourself?

If you said yes (or even had to think about it for a bit), um, well, hmmmm...

That's kinda like saying you're too busy driving to stop for gas. Makes no sense. And, whether you *want* to stop for gas or not, drive long enough and you'll *need* to.

Same thing with life. If we ignore our emotional/physical fuel gauge and just keep driving and driving and driving, sooner or later we're gonna run out of gas. And, rather than the annoying (and embarrassing) call for help and/or walk to the gas station, we find ourselves laid out in bed and/or in the hospital (or worse).

If you think you're too busy to take care of yourself, you REALLY need to take care of yourself.

Whether that's developing a regular meditation practice, going to the gym five times a week, getting a massage once a week or reading in the bath more often, we all need to fill up.

So, quit being a martyr, say no to some of the stuff

that just *isn't* really that important, and take care of yourself.

Oh, one more thing. Ever hear the story about the guy who runs into another guy who's sawing down a tree? He's watching the guy work and work and work and he's like: *"Hey, dood. You might want to sharpen that saw. I think it'll make everything a lot easier."* And the other guy says: *"No way, man. I'm way too busy to slow down long enough to sharpen this thing."*

Don't be that silly sawing guy. (Pretty, please.)

NO MORE ICE CUBES, PLEASE

If you had a boiling pot of water and you wanted to easily and permanently make the water stop boiling, would you:

A) Drop in two ice cubes at regular intervals; or,

B) Turn the flame off/move the pot off the heat?

Unless you're insane, you'd pick option B, eh? Seems so simple... Yet, somehow, in a world where 15 million+ peeps have purchased Stephen Covey's *The 7 Habits of Highly Effective People*, we've failed to implement Habit #1 to "Be Proactive."

Instead, we throw our hands up in the air at all the symptoms we experience (from acid reflux to depression) and, rather than go after the *causes* of these ailments, we reach for another couple ice cubes to temporarily reduce the heat while doing *nothing* to deal with the flame at the root of the underlying problem.

bizarre

How 'bout you. Do *you* ever do that? What ~~bottle of pills~~ ice cube tray are you relying on and what can you do to deal with the cause of the issue?!

EXERCISE VS. ZOLOFT

Did you know exercise is scientifically proven to be as effective as Zoloft in reducing depression?

Yep.[32]

Here's the study: Scientists took a bunch of clinically depressed peeps and randomly assigned them to three groups. For four months, one group exercised, one group took an antidepressant (Zoloft), and another group tried exercise + Zoloft.

The exercise group participated in three forty-five minute supervised workouts per week consisting of cycling or walking/jogging at moderate to high intensity.

At the end of the four months, ALL three groups showed significant improvements in their well-being— with exercise proving to be *just as effective* as the antidepressant!

And get this: When the researchers checked in six months later, the exercise group was significantly less likely to have relapsed into depression than the medication group.

THAT. IS. HUGE.

Makes you wonder why the results of THAT "clinical trial" aren't advertised on every other commercial, eh? Must be because anything worth advertising has to have a frightening list of possible side effects... ;)

Seriously, though.

steps up on soap box

EXERCISE!

Please. Pretty please.

Our bodies were made to move and exercise has gotta be *the* cheapest insurance policy against terminal funkiness out there.

---

32 Picked this up from Sonja Lyubomirsky's *brilliant* book, *The How of Happiness*, where she cites the 1999 study from the Archives of Internal Medicine. Check out the PhilosophersNote and get her phenomenal book for more.

CONSISTENCY OVER INTENSITY

After I sold my first business (eteamz), I had enough cash to take a couple years to figure out what I wanted to do when I grew up. I quickly realized that I was committed to studying and living universal truths of optimal living while inspiring others to do the same. I also quickly realized that if I had a hard time getting out of bed in the morning I was going to have a hard time living at my highest potential.

So, I decided to study how to optimize my energy. I figured going thru the certification process to become a personal trainer would be a good way to introduce myself to the subject.

I learned some cool stuff. The #1 thing that stuck with me the most: *Consistency over intensity.*

Think about it this way: When most people get into fitness they're ALL ABOUT IT—hitting the gym (or track or yoga class or trail or whatever) hard for a couple hours, feeling all geeked up about life and their extraordinary commitment to really crushing it this time.

That commitment lasts right up until the next morning when they're so sore they can't get out of bed. Ouch.

So, the idea is this: It's WAY better to simply put on your shoes, head out and do a nice, mellow workout CONSISTENTLY then it is to go all gonzo and then never go back.

Consistency over intensity.

(Of course, it doesn't need to be either/or and consistent intensity (with "intense" rest phases) is grand. But, if you're not consistent yet, focus on that before you go for all the marbles, yo! :)

THE TRAINING EFFECT

The #2 coolest thing I learned was the science behind how our bodies actually get stronger. In exercise physiology parlance, the process is called "The Training Effect." It goes something like this:

First, we need to "Overload" our bodies—we need to go past our current comfort zones and, basically, ask our body to work a little harder than it's used to working. (Not *too* far past the comfort zone or we're likely to injure ourselves. Think "Stretch Zone" not "Snap Zone.")

Now, our bodies are remarkably adaptive and don't like getting their butts kicked and they basically say, *"Hey, there! Wow. So, uh, you want me to be able to lift that weight / run that extra mile / swim that extra lap, eh? Well, alrighty then. Bring it on!"*

After that little self-pep-talk, our bodies "Overcompensate"—they strengthen themselves so they can handle that new level of stress next time around. Pretty cool, eh?

What's *really* cool is that the training effect applies to EVERY aspect of our lives.

If we want to get better at great communication (whether it's in the boardroom or in the bedroom), we've gotta go just past our current edge, "overloading" ourselves with a *little* more than we're currently comfie with. Same basic thing goes for learning a new language or a musical instrument or meditation practice or...

So, how about a little training?!

P.S. Gotta drop a little William James love here. He reminds us: *"You have enormous untapped power you'll probably never tap, because most people never run far enough on their first wind to ever find they have a second."*

P.P.S. Here's to tapping that enormous power!

JUST WONDERING

Just wondering: Why is it OK/totally normal to eat chicken nuggets and hot dogs (do you know what's *in those?!* ack!) as we drink beer by the case and party all night long while it's weird to drink green juice and eat whole foods and get up early for meditation?

scratches head

I guess it's not all *that* surprising. What would you expect from a world where more people are overweight than underfed and where we take antidepressants like they're tic-tacs?

P.S. Did you know that, in 2004, 66% of the US population was overweight or obese? Yah. Prolly don't want to be "normal" in a society like that, huh?

P.P.S. I guess that's why Krishnamurti tells us: *"It's no measure of health to be well adjusted to a profoundly sick society."*

BLOODLETTING &
MODERN MEDICINE

Did you know George Washington was drained of half his blood before he died of complications from strep throat? Yep.

Is it just me or is that *weird?*

Hard to believe that some of *the* most brilliant, successful and respected allopathic doctors of his era (remember: this was only 200 years ago!), were convinced that bleeding this great man of half (!) his blood was the absolute best way to "cure" him.

scratches head

Seems a little barbaric from today's perspective, eh?

You might want to keep that in mind the next time you accept the Almighty proclamations of your extremely well-educated, invariably well-intentioned, yet often remarkably misguided Doctor.

And, please join me in a silent prayer that it doesn't take another 200 years for our current methods of treating cancer (cut the tumor out! poison her with chemotherapy and radiation!), heart disease (saw open his breast plate and inflate the arteries!) and diabetes (cut off that annoying limb as we watch him go blind!) to be seen in the same barbaric light as good ol' bloodletting.

P.S. Of course, I'm not against all instances of sophisticated invasive responses to advanced health challenges, but here's the REALLY annoying part: We already have a cure for the stuff that's killing us. It's called a healthy immune system. Unfortunately, it's not nearly as profitable (for those seeking immediate profits at the expense of the greater economy and our world's well-being) to sell a new set of lifestyle choices rather than another bottle of pills or expensive, cutting-edge "treatments."

P.P.S. One more thing: Did you know we can *easily* cure most cases of Type II diabetes in days? Yep. Just get someone off all the stuff that's causing the insulin imbalance (sugar, animal products, refined foods) and get them eating what our bodies were made to consume (an abundance of nutritionally dense whole foods) then add some exercise and *Voilà!* Diabetes is cured. Unfortunately, because they haven't found a (profitable) little pill that can magically solve the problem, the medical industry has deemed diabetes "incurable."

WHY AREN'T MORE PEOPLE INFURIATED BY THAT NONSENSE?!? Ahem.

P.P.P.S. Same rant applies to heart "disease." Why we'd rather have radical surgeries than quit eating the stuff that's killing us is baffling. Very baffling.

scratches head again

steps off soapbox (for now)

SUBSIDIZING SICKNESS

You ever wonder why a hamburger at Mickey D's costs less than a head of romaine lettuce?

Strange, no?

You may not know it, but you're actually subsidizing the production of that hamburger and keeping it nice and cheap. Yep. Every year we all chip in billions of dollars in subsidies that go into the production of corn and soybeans[33] that're fed to the (factory-farmed) animals that get (inhumanely) slaughtered and served to us through the local drive thru.

Now, if those hamburgers were nourishing us, those subsidies might not be all *that* bad. But, we *scientifically know* that the overconsumption of animal products is one of THE primary causes of all the diseases that're crippling our world. It's literally insane. We're subsidizing the creation of sickness.

What's most ironic (and incredibly annoying) is the fact that we're not only subsidizing the destruction of our health we're also subsidizing the "cure" of these ailments that could have been avoided in the first place.

Well, at least the meat and dairy factory farms and pharmaceutical industries are profiting enormously at our collective expense as they destroy the environment, eh?

Grrr...

I say it's time for us to pull our heads out of our collective butts and do something about this. Like now.

---

33 Check out Whole Foods Market CEO John Mackey's essay on "Taxpayers" in Moby and Miyun Park's great book *Gristle: From Factory Farms to Food Safety – Thinking Twice about the Meat We Eat.*

THE GODDESSES OF WEALTH

Deepak[34] tells a story about the two Goddesses of wealth, Lakshmi and Saraswati. It goes something like this:

Lakshmi is the traditional Goddess of Wealth. The problem is, if you go straight after her (by constantly chasing the bling) she'll tend to avoid you.

Saraswati's the Goddess of Knowledge. If you go after *her* (by pursuing self-knowledge, wisdom and all that goodness), an interesting thing happens. Apparently, Lakshmi's a jealous Goddess. If she sees you flirting with Saraswati she'll chase after you.

Now, I'm a one-Goddess kinda guy (and her name is Alexandra), but I like that story.

---

34 This is from Deepak's great little book *Creating Affluence*. Love it.

TRUST-FUND BABIES

Although I wasn't born with a silver spoon in my mouth or with a sweet trust fund waiting for me, I was blessed to have parents who taught me the virtue of showing up, working hard and serving.

But, I kinda always wished I was born into a blissload of wealth. :)

One day I came up with the idea that the Universe/ World/Whatever is a sort of über-parent—with infinite wealth and a huge trust fund for me (and all of us).

Now, the cool thing about this trust fund is that it provides all we need—with one nice little caveat: The cash comes flowin' out only to the extent we show up— diligently, patiently, persistently and playfully giving ourselves to the world.

Makes me feel great to know I have such a nice little trust fund and such a reliable way to tap into it.

CLEANING UP THE GREMLIN POOP

Quick science lesson: Your brain has four primary states: Beta (active thinking), Alpha (mellow chill-axing), Theta (REM sleep) and Delta (deep dreamless sleep).

When you're super stressed, you're hanging out in high Beta, with cortisol and adrenalin and all the other stress gremlins out in force—weakening your immune system and overall mojo. Unfortunately, with the busy-ness of our modern lives, we spend *way* too much time in this "fight-or-flight" stress-mode and our minds and bodies take a beating because of it.

Research unequivocally shows that simple medita-tion practices for as little as 12-15 minutes a day can have HUGE positive results for us. As we close our eyes, breathe deeply and allow our minds to chillax, we go from Beta to Alpha while triggering what Herbert Benson (the preeminent Harvard MD/researcher) calls "The Relaxation Response."

When we hang out there, all the gremlin poop can be cleaned up and our health/vitality nurtured. So... You taking the time to scoop the gremlin poop?

STRENGTH TRAINING
FOR YOUR BRAIN

Did you know that in Pali (the old-school language of Buddha's day), they don't even have a word for meditation?

Nopesicles. The closest they have is *bhavana*[35]—which literally means something like "consciousness training" and refers to the disciplined, rigorous training required to shape our minds in order to become better, more conscious/healthy/awesome human beings.

I like to think of meditation/*bhavana* as hitting the gym for our brains. When I find my mind wandering during my meditation (as it often likes to do), as I bring my focus back to my breath, I imagine doing another bicep curl or bench press for my mind. I'm getting a little stronger… a little stronger… and a little more likely to have the strength to step into the gap between stimulus and response during my day-to-day life.

Then I can more consistently choose an empowered response to any given situation and be the type of person I aspire to be.

P.S. I love to imagine His Holiness the 14th Dalai Lama's (HHDL) consciousness looking like Arnold

Schwarzenegger's body—all yolked out and ripped and money. :)

P.P.S. Did you know that if HHDL has a *really* busy day scheduled, he'll meditate for two hours instead of one? That's hot.

P.P.P.S. Technically, meditation is more like *samadhi* training for our minds than strength training for our minds.

Samadhi's an awesome word. It means "one-pointed-ness." As we develop our *samadhi* muscles, we cultivate control of our minds such that we can put our attention where we want, when we want. Fact is, without a great deal of *samadhi*, it's *impossible* to live consciously!!!

So, (in Arnold-voice): Here's to pumping *samadhi*-iron, yo!!

---

35 Picked this word goodness up from Jon Kabat-Zinn's fantastic *Wherever You Go, There You Are.*

"As an irrigator guides water to his fields, as an archer aims an arrow, as a carpenter carves wood, the wise shape their lives."
— Buddha

"Do not be impatient with your seemingly slow progress. Do not try to run faster than you presently can. If you are studying, reflecting and trying, you are making progress whether you are aware of it or not. A traveler walking the road in the darkness of night is still going forward. Someday, some way, everything will... break open, like the natural unfolding of a rosebud."
— Vernon Howard

"There is about wisdom a nobility and magnificence in the fact that she doesn't just fall to a person's lot, that each man owes her to his own efforts, that one doesn't go to anyone other than oneself to find her."
— Seneca

"It seems that the necessary thing to do is not to fear mistakes, to plunge in, to do the best that one can, hoping to learn enough from blunders to correct them eventually."
— Abraham Maslow

"What is to give light must endure burning."
— Viktor Frankl

WISDOM

Wisdom is all about taking what
we know and making that the essence of who we are as we see
life as our classroom and every
moment as another opportunity to
live with more
integrity.

THE 12 HOWS OF HAPPINESS

People often ask me what *one* book I'd recommend if they could only read one book. (Before I wrote this book ;) I had a hard time answering that question until I read Sonja Lyubomirsky's brilliant *The How of Happiness*[36] where she outlines the 12 scientifically proven ways we can boost our happiness.

We touch on most of them in various ways throughout this little book. Here they are:

1. Expressing Gratitude

2. Cultivating Optimism

3. Avoiding Overthinking and Social Comparison

4. Practicing Acts of Kindness

5. Nurturing Social Relationships

6. Developing Strategies for Coping

7. Learning to Forgive

8. Increasing Flow Experiences

9. Savoring Life's Joys

10. Committing to Your Goals

11. Practicing Religion and Spirituality

12. Taking Care of Your Body: Meditation + Physical Activity + Acting Like a Happy Person

P.S. One of the coolest points Dr. L makes in the book is the fact that, as we decide what happiness practices to focus on, we want to avoid the "shoulds" and pick the ones that *really* inspire us! Why? Well, we're *much* more likely to stick to the intrinsic goals that have deep personal meaning!

P.P.S. So, as you get inspired by all the Ideas in this book, focus on the ones that REALLY light you up! Not the ones you think you *should* do. Cool? Cool. (And, while we're on the subject: What are your favorite Ideas so far? How can you integrate them into your life?!)

---

36 This book seriously rocks. Especially if you're into Positive Psych like I am. Check it out and/or check out the PhilosophersNote on it.

ACTING LIKE A HAPPY PERSON

You might've noticed the 12th How of Happiness included "Acting Like a Happy Person." Really? *That's* a scientifically proven way to increase our happiness? Yep.

Simply *acting like* a happy person is enough to boost your well-being.

As David Reynolds[37] puts it: *"Behavior wags the tail of feelings... We do, then we feel."* In other words: *"Feelings follow behavior."*

Too often when we feel like crapola, we just want to curl up in bed and ignore the world, hygiene habits and everything else. Tragically, that's the *worst* thing we can do in those moments. The reality is that if we simply *acted like* a happy person would act, we're likely to *feel* like a happy person would feel.

So, if you find yourself feeling funky, quit slouching over, breathing shallowly and repeating to yourself how much your life sucks. Although it might sound cheesy, there's science (and common sense) that tells us that those moments are exactly when we need to stand up straight, shake ourselves out, put our shoulders back, breathe deeply and walk with a confident smile as we remind ourselves we got it goin' on.

P.S. You also might've noticed the #1 happiness practice: "Expressing Gratitude"—which is *THE* easiest way to boost our mood. Research has shown that simply keeping a weekly gratitude journal[38] where you capture stuff you're grateful for (from the mundane to the sublime) significantly boosts your happiness levels compared to those who don't. So, what are you grateful for today?

---

37 Highly recommend Reynolds' *Constructive Living*. Awesome book.

---

38 Check out http://www.GratitudeLog.com where thousands of cool peeps are capturing their gratitude on a regular basis! Good stuff.

ACTING AS IF

While we're on the subject, I've gotta say I've always had a bit of an allergy to the whole "Act as if"/"Fake it till you make it" pom-pom stuff. Felt more than a little sketchy/inauthentic/lame-ola for me.

But Wayne Dyer has a great way to approach the whole "Acting as if" dealio that I really love. It goes something like this:

Imagine aspects of your ideal self—whether it's being an awesome parent or being in incredible physical shape or being a great spouse or being an über-creative artist/entrepreneur (or whatever it is for you).

Now, imagine you're facing a challenge in one of those domains and you're not quite feeling like doing the right thing—your kids are being out of control and you're about to yell at them, you've put on some extra weight and your energy sucks yet you don't feel like eating well/going to the gym like you said you would, your spouse is annoying you and you're getting snappy, you're feeling overwhelmed professionally and are about to avoid doing what needs to be done as you get your procrastination on, etc.

Alright. Now, as you're experiencing that challenge, take a moment and imagine your ideal self and think about how *that* version of you would show up in that situation.

The rock star parent would probably take a deep breath, smile and apply that sweet parenting tip you just learned, eh?

The amazing spouse version of you would take a deep breath and try to see your Love's perspective and settle down while the über-radiantly alive version of you would head to the gym and have a great workout and the creative genius version of you would realize fear is an inevitable part of any project and the greatest among us simply take the next step and do what needs to be done. Yah?

So, there ya go. Next time you're feeling your less-than-stellar self starting to run the show, pause for a moment, reflect on what your Highest Self would do and then act as if you *already* were that super cool version of you. Good times are guaranteed to ensue.

STATES & TRAITS

Doesn't it feel great to walk on fire and just *know* you can do anything you really set your mind to? And what about that amazing energy you feel after a yoga (or meditation or whatever) retreat? Or how about that ineffable bliss of falling in love?

Gotta love those (state) experiences, eh?

And...

How about the inevitable crashes that follow? Aren't *those* a blast?! ;)

Here's the deal: It's *really* easy to get all geeked up about pretty much anything for a weekend or a week or a honeymoon. It's an *entirely* different thing to actually LIVE from that place.

Ken Wilber describes the process as turning "states" of experience into "traits" of who we are.

And that takes work. Diligent, patient, persistent and playful work. Day in and day out. Week in and week out.

Month in and month out. Year in and year out. Decade in and decade out. But that doesn't sell does it?

SPIRAL DYNAMICS

Ever heard of "Spiral Dynamics"?[39] Here's the quick overview: People and cultures go through different stages of development. The Spiral guys like to color-code them to make it easier to keep track. It goes something like this:

RED. Think: Terrible twos. I'll blow you up if you piss me off. (Yikes!)

BLUE. Think: Ten Commandments. Fundamentalist anything. Rules are paramount. Literal interpretations of the Bible are absolutely correct.

ORANGE. Think: Wall Street. Academia. Science and ambition are key here.

GREEN. Think: Environmentalism. Pluralism. All is one. Non-violent.

So, the idea is that we evolve through these stages of development. All of those stages above are part of what they call the "first tier." Here's the funny thing about those perspectives: they're all convinced they're *100%* right. It's a big food fight.

GREEN looks at ORANGE and says, *"You greedy capitalists!!! You're good for nothing and totally destroying our planet! And, my non-violent self HATES you!"*

ORANGE looks at GREEN and says, *"You tree-hugging, New Agey hippies!! Get a job and contribute to the economy, will ya?!? And quit gazing at those crystals."*

BLUE looks at everyone and says, *"You're all going to hell because you don't believe in [insert favorite God here]!!"*

RED looks at everyone and says, *"You don't agree with me? Fine. I'm blowin' you up."*

Everything is "either, or." No one can see the validity of the other perspectives. Not so good. The ideal? Let's consciously evolve as individuals and as a culture to a "second-tier" level of consciousness. Here, for the first time, we can hold multiple perspectives. We can see that, in Ken Wilber's words: *"No one is smart enough to be 100% wrong."*:)

What's that look like? Well, we can see the truth in the need to take care of our environment AND the need for a powerful economy AND the need for rules and regulations AND the need to take aggressive action when the situation demands it.

Every stage has a PARTIAL truth. To embrace the whole we need to transcend AND include and start saying "yes, and..." a lot more than "either, or..." Powerful schtuff.

---

39 Spiral Dynamics = Very cool stuff integrated into Ken Wilber's work and developed by Don Beck and Chris Cowan from the work of Clare Graves. (That's a mouthful! :)

HIGHER HIGHS
& HIGHER LOWS

Here's the deal: We're never going to be happy *all* the time. Anyone who tells you they are is lying (either to you or themselves or both).

Dan Millman[40] says there are no enlightened beings—only more or less enlightened moments. I love that.

Everything in nature (including our emotions!) has its rhythms—day and night, high tide and low tide, spring/summer/fall/winter.

The good news is that as we choose to step forward into growth and actually live our truths more and more consistently, what we'll find is that our highs get higher AND our lows get higher—such that our new "off" days are often better than our former best days.

The key (that unlocks all doors)?

Diligently, patiently, persistently and playfully live our ideals and, in the long run (!), our highs will be higher and so will our lows. And that rocks.

---

40 This idea is from Dan's *Everyday Enlightenment*—which rocks. Dan was one of the first authors I loved so much I read everything he wrote. Check out *Way of the Peaceful Warrior, Living on Purpose* and *Body Mind Mastery* as well!

OUR EMOTIONAL
GUIDANCE SYSTEM

Esther & Jerry Hicks[41] tell us that our emotions are kinda like our car's fuel gauge—measuring just how connected we are to good ol' Source.

When we're feeling great (loving/appreciative/empowered/joyful), we're connected to the Divine within us. Tank is full. All good. When we're feeling all depressed/helpless/disempowered, that's basically our emotional guidance system/fuel gauge telling us we're on "E"—disconnected from the highest within us. Eek.

Now, the Hicks' make the very important point that, if we're driving our car and notice we're approaching "E," we don't whine and moan and get all up in our stuff. We simply pull over at the next gas station and fill up. Yah?

They say we should approach our emotions the same way. If we're feeling all cranky-saurus-rex, we just need to notice we're approaching "E" and simply *FILL UP!!* by pulling over at the nearest Source energy station (aka, doing whatever it is that makes us feel most connected to our Highest Selves—whether that's dancing, meditation, walking, running, hiking, yoga, tai-chi, playing with our babies, cuddling with our Love or whatever!).

Now, personally, when I drive our sweet little Prius around I don't like to let it get lower than a ¼ tank as I'm not a huge fan of worrying about running out of gas in the middle of the road.

SAME THING WITH MY LIFE.

I've run out of emotional gas one too many times and now I pretty much like to top off that ol' tank daily—starting with my AM meditation, journaling and exercise and ending with my PM meditation and appreciations. It's REALLY (!!!) hard for me to have a really bad day when I make sure the tank is close to full. Highly recommend it.

How 'bout you? You driving near "E" way too often?

What are your key fill-'er-up practices you can rock to stay connected and feeling great?!

---

41 I'm still a little freaked out by the fact that Esther channels a group of beings collectively called "Abraham" (huh? :) but I've gotten over that weirdness b/c the wisdom they share is so often great. This metaphor of Emotional Fuel Gauges runs throughout their work and, if you're feelin' it, I highly recommend their best-sellers *Ask & It is Given, The Amazing Power of Deliberate Intent,* and *Money, and the Law of Attraction.* Check out the PhilosophersNotes on all of those books.

QUADRANT IV
—> QUADRANT II

Stephen Covey has a handy-dandy four quadrant model for effective self-/time-management that's a key part of his 3rd Habit to "Put First Things First."

As you may know, the basic idea is that activities can be categorized as either Urgent or Not Urgent and Important or Not Important and we can throw those possibilities into that little four quadrant model.

Quadrant II is for the Important but Not Urgent goodness and includes things like meditation, quality time with your family, working out, yoga, hiking, journaling, studying, etc.

Basically, stuff that renews your soul.

Quadrant IV, on the other hand, is for the Not Important and Not Urgent distractions and includes time-wasting stuff like checking ESPN for the 100th time that day (my personal favorite), flipping aimlessly thru the 2.43 million channels on TV or spending hours surfing the Internet.

Now, I've noticed I tend to fall into Quadrant IV time-wasting activities when I'm stressed/overwhelmed/

avoiding something/etc. and I've created a little game where I try to catch myself when I'm stuck in Q-IV. I see if I can swap that Q-IV soul-sucking activity for a Q-II soul-nourishing one. It's quite cool.

So, for example, when I'm about to load the ESPN page to see the same updates from the last time I checked 10 minutes ago, I can notice it and say, *"Aha! Nice try, dood. You're burned out at the moment and need a little break, yo. What's a cool Q-II you can rock that would make you feel great rather than like a weenie? Ohhh... Yah. Good idea. Let's go for a hike."*

Feel free to change up the internal monologue but give it a shot if you're feelin' it the next time you start your Q-IV slide! :)

SPIN CYCLES

You ever stress yourself out so badly that you just spin and spin a problem in your head, trying to figure out the best solution without getting anywhere?

I've mastered that process and call it "The Spin Cycle." Not fun.

At a certain point, there's no way anything good's going to come out of any more thinking and we've just gotta let it go—ideally doing *anything* other than continuing the spin cycle.

My personal favorite way to deal with it is an awesome hike but, whatever, we do, the idea is simple: We've gotta learn to notice the spin cycle and pop out of it.

P.S. Psychologists call this "ruminating." In Sonja Lyubomirsky's words: *"The combination of rumination and negative mood is toxic."* And, *"If you are someone plagued by ruminations, you are unlikely to become happier before you can break that habit."*

So, let's break the spin cycle habit!!

MIS-TAKES, BAGELS, PERFECTION & FLYING

Michael Beckwith tells us that even enlightened beings burn their bagels on occasion. Rumi tells us that there is no worse pretense than the pretense of perfection. Maslow tells us that there are, in fact, no perfect human beings.[42]

I often consult their wisdom when I find myself all up in my stuff b/c I just did something silly or when I'm struggling with something that was so clear (!) just the other day.

Here's some Rumi goodness that's great for those days when you're giving yourself a hard time cuz you should've already figured it out: *"God turns you from one feeling to another and teaches by means of opposites, so that you will have two wings to fly, not one."*

Beckwith cooking wisdom for when you're burning stuff: *"A conscious realization of our innate oneness with the Ineffable does not mean that we will never make a mistake again. Even enlightened beings burn their bagels once in a while. It's important to maintain a sense of humor because this is how you will stop being afraid of making a mistake. You'll make some, but so what? That's why they're called mis-takes. Humor relaxes the uptight ego. You get* a new cue from your inner Self and simply say, 'I missed my cue, so let's do a second take.' Your willingness to take the risk of making a mistake is actually an expression of courage and a willingness to grow from them. Mistakes are about getting the blessing in the lesson and the lesson in the blessing."

(Isn't that "mis-take" line genius? LOVE that!)

And, Maslow seals the deal: "There are no perfect human beings! Persons can be found who are good, very good indeed, in fact, great. There do in fact exist creators, seers, sages, saints, shakers, and movers... even if they are uncommon and do not come by the dozen. And yet these very same people can at times be boring, irritating, petulant, selfish, angry or depressed. To avoid disillusionment with human nature, we must first give up our illusions about it."

Boom!

---

42 Beckwith from *Spiritual Liberation* + Rumi from *Rumi Daylight* + Maslow from *Motivation & Personality*. PhilosophersNotes available on all.

GUIDING STARS
& DISTANT SHORES

Are you, like me, a perfectionist? If so, please sit up straight and pay attention. I think you'll really like this one.

You know those ideals you have for yourself? All the things you want to be and just *know* you could be if you *really* lived with Integrity and Mojo and all the Divine Virtue you're capable of rockin'?!

Well, Tal Ben-Shahar (yah, him again—I told you he's one of my favorites these days) tells us it's a LOT healthier to imagine those ideals as GUIDING STARS and *not* as distant shores we may someday reach.

Fact is, we perfectionists with those über-(silly-at-times) goals are NEVER (!!!) gonna "get there" (where the heck is "there" anyway?).

Those ideals? They're *guiding stars.* NOT, I repeat, distant shores.

P.S. Tal calls Perfectionists who get the above wisdom "Optimalists"—they deal with the constraints of their reality to *optimize* their lives rather than try to create the impossibly perfect. Powerful stuff.

P.P.S. Psychologist Carl Rogers described it this way: *"The good life is a process, not a state of being. It is a direction, not a destination."* How beautiful is *that*?!

"Anyone who says he isn't afraid of anything is both stupid and lying."
— David Reynolds

"God will not have his work made manifest by cowards."
— Ralph Waldo Emerson

*"Our doubts are traitors, and make us lose the good
we oft might win, by fearing to attempt."*
— William Shakespeare

*"Courage is resistance to fear,
mastery of fear—not absence of fear."*
— Mark Twain

*"Fear is the cheapest room in the house.
I would like to see you living in better conditions."*
— Hafez

*"Fear is the mind-killer.
Fear is the little-death that brings total obliteration.
I will face my fear. I will permit it to pass over me
and through me. And when it has gone past,
I will turn the inner eye to see its path.
Where the fear has gone there will be nothing.
Only I will remain."*
— Frank Herbert

*"Only those who risk going too far
can possibly find out how far they can go."*
— T.S. Eliot

*"There is only one thing that makes
a dream impossible to achieve: the fear of failure."*
— Paulo Coelho

COURAGE

It's not about getting rid of all our fears. It's about feeling the fear and then doing what needs to be done.

THE HEART OF VIRTUE

Did you know the word *courage* comes from the French and Latin words for "heart"?

Yeppers.

And, just as the heart is the organ that pumps blood to our arms and legs and other organs, courage is the virtue that vitalizes all the other virtues.

Fact is, without courage, all the other virtues whither away into, as psychologist Rollo May tells us, "mere facsimiles of virtue" and all this fancy pants stuff we're talking about dissolves into meaningless intellectual abstraction (and the resulting spiritual farts).

So, we've gotta get our courage on.

Let's look at some ways to do that, shall we?

ARISTOTLE'S COURAGE

First thing to know is that it's not about having *no* fear. It's about having courage. There's a big difference.

Aristotle puts it brilliantly.

He describes a "virtuous mean"—the middle path between the "vice of deficiency" (not having *enough* of a virtue) and the "vice of excess" (having *too much* of a virtue).

In his handy-dandy model, we've got the virtue of courage—the noble quality that gives us the mojo to move ahead in the face of fear. We're freaked out, but we go for it anyway.

Now, if I'm a bit of a tough guy about it and have *too much* courage, I'm gonna suffer from a *vice of excess* that Aristotle calls "rashness." I might just jump out of an airplane without a parachute or something equally (un)wise.

On the other hand, if I'm overwhelmed by fear/have too little courage, I'm going to have a *vice of deficiency.* In other words: I'm a coward.

So, the trick is to allow ourselves to feel the fear, check in to see what the most prudent course of action is and then go ahead and do what needs to be done (which, of course, might be *not* jumping out of that plane!).

Here's to the virtuous mean!

FEAR & EXPECTATIONS

Are you afraid of something right now?

Pause for a moment and identify one thing that's kinda (or really) stressing you out. Might be that you'll never figure out your purpose in life, tonight's date might suck, you won't be able to pay the rent next month, the world's going to implode, kids are gonna grow up to be criminals. Whatever.

Got it?

All right. Now, I can *guarantee* you that your fear is tied to a NEGATIVE EXPECTATION. You think something's gonna go wrong. Perhaps *really* wrong.

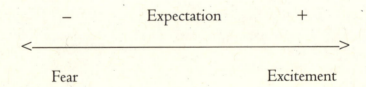

Good news. There's a remarkably simple (though not always *easy*) way to fix it. We've gotta shift from that negative expectation to a more positive one.[43] As we do that, we shift from fear to excitement. Sounds simple.

And, well, it is. (The trick, of course, is actually *doing* this when the fear gremlins invade our minds!!)

Let's identify the negative expectation that's producing your fear and see if we can create a more positive expectation and, if you're feeling spicy, let's imagine something so positive that you actually get excited.

My negative expectation:_____

_____

_____

A more positive expectation:_____

_____

_____

A super positive expectation:_____

_____

There ya go. Fear and expectations.

To recap: If you're feeling fear, check in on what you're expecting to happen. It's negative. To shift from fear to faith to excitement, shift your expectations from really bad to OK to great. Powerful stuff.

---

43 Shout out to Jose Silva and Burt Goldman for introducing me to this brilliant idea in their great little book *The Silva Mind Control Method of Mental Dynamics.*

DRAGONS & LIZARDS

Hero's journey traveler tip: When faced with the inevitable challenges that arise as we push our edges and see what we're capable of in this precious little life of ours, it's helpful to remember that the hero battles big, ugly, stinky, fire-breathing *dragons.* Not lizards.

If there weren't obstacles to overcome and demons to face, everyone would do it and it would be called "an average person's journey" not "a hero's journey," eh?

So, if you're getting your butt kicked around a bit, know that's just part of the deal. Take a deep breath, appreciate your audacity and go back to giving it your best shot.

(And, if all you're ever doing is side-stepping lizards, you might want to turn it up a notch or three. Just sayin'.)

THE MAGIC SHIELD

I haven't read it myself yet, but apparently there's an awesome story in John Bunyan's *Pilgrim's Progress* about a guy with a magic shield.

Get this: The hero of this little story has a shield that makes him invincible. There's just one condition. Our hero has to face his problems/challenges head on— with the shield in front of him. He does that and he's *invincible.* If, on the other hand, he gets a little freaked out and runs away from/avoids his challenges, he's suddenly vulnerable. D'oh.

Question: Are you avoiding anything in *your* life?

Suggestion: Pick up your shield and head toward your fears!

THE ULTIMATE JIHAD

Did you know the word *jihad* comes from the Arabic word for "struggle" and that there are actually two kinds of jihads or struggles?

Yep. One struggle is against *external* oppressors and one is WITHIN OURSELVES—the battle between our higher and lower selves.

Guess which one is known as the "greater holy war"?

Bingo. The struggle within *ourselves.* The battle between the good and the evil within our own being is, easily, the greatest struggle there is.

All the great traditions talk about it.

The Bhagavad Gita, a core text of Hinduism, is set on a metaphorical battlefield and features a reluctant warrior receiving Divine counsel to do the battle necessary to conquer his lower self and live his dharma.

While Proverbs 16:32 tells us: *"He who rules his spirit has won a greater victory than the taking of a city."*

And Lao-tzu tells us: *"Mastering others is strength; mastering yourself is true power."*

And, the Buddha tells us: *"One who conquers himself is greater than another who conquers a thousand times a thousand men on the battlefield."*

And, finally, Muhammad himself says: *"The most excellent Jihad is that for the conquest of self."*

Ultimately, it's all about self-mastery. Let's show up fully in the most holy of wars as we truly live the ideals in which we so passionately believe. We all do that and the "other" wars will dissolve.

"Love is our highest word and the synonym for God."
— Ralph Waldo Emerson

*"If he desired to know about automobiles, he would,
without question, study diligently about automobiles.
If his wife desired to be a gourmet cook, she'd certainly study
the art of cooking, perhaps even attending a cooking class.
Yet, it never seems as obvious to him that if he wants
to live in love, he must spend at least as much time
as the auto mechanic or the gourmet in studying love."*
— Leo Buscaglia

"To say 'I love you' one must know first how to say the 'I.'"
— Ayn Rand

*"From the standpoint of daily life, however, there is one
thing we do know: that we are here for the sake of each other—
above all for those upon whose smile and well-being our own
happiness depends, and also for the countless unknown souls
with whose fate we are connected by a bond of sympathy.
Many times a day I realize how much my own outer
and inner life is built upon the labors of my fellow men,
both living and dead, and how earnestly I must exert
myself in order to give in return as much as I have received."*
— Albert Einstein

*"Strive constantly to serve the welfare of the world;
by devotion to selfless work one attains the supreme goal of life.
Do your work with the welfare of others always in mind."*
— Krishna

*"Let your one delight and refreshment be to pass from one
service to the community to another, with God ever in mind."*
— Marcus Aurelius

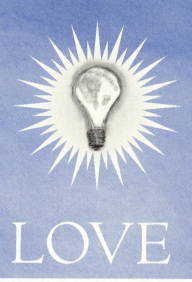

LOVE

All the other stuff without love? Not worth a whole lot. Love starts with ourselves and needs to be approached like anything else we want to **master**—with a lot of diligent studying and practicing!

5:1 - THE MAGIC # OF LOVE

John Gottman can bring a married couple into his lab and, after watching them interact for a matter of minutes, can predict with 90%+ accuracy whether they'll stay together or divorce.

How's he do it?

He measures the ratio of positive to negative interactions between the couple (do they criticize one another or say something kind? move away from one another or touch each other lovingly?) and has found that couples that thrive have at least 5 positive interactions to every 1 negative interaction.

5:1. It's the magic number of love.

Knowing this, my Wife/Goddess/Love and I have a little ritual. Every night before we go to bed we swap appreciations with one another—at least 5 things we really appreciate about the other—from little things like *"I appreciate you making us green juice today"* to appreciating each other's top strengths (Alexandra's are: Playfulness, Gratitude, Creativity, Hope & Optimism, Curiosity/ Love of Learning, and Wisdom).

It's a *REALLY* cool way to fall asleep and helps us make sure we're rockin' the 5:1. When we have kids we're planning to play The Appreciation Game with them as we tuck 'em in. Good times!

Here's to Love Magic.

P.S. Speaking of appreciation, check this out: When you appreciate someone, their value appreciates. That's cool.

OVERDOSING ON SEROTONIN

Ever heard about the effects of kindness on your brain? It goes something like this:[44]

Serotonin makes you feel good. It's one of the drugs the pharmaceutical companies pump into those wonderful little antidepressants. It's also a little drug God decided to pump through our brains when we do things He/She/It likes—kinda like a little reward for good behavior.

Here's what's cool: When you do something kind for someone, the person you're helping has serotonin released in her brain—she feels happier. And, so do you.

Pretty sweet, eh? Two more serotonin-induced happier people in the world! Yayuh!

Perhaps the most incredible thing is this: Not only do you and the person you helped feel better, so does some random person who happened to watch your act of kindness. That's amazing.

So, uh, how 'bout a little serotonin overdose today?!

---

44 Picked this up from Wayne Dyer in his great book *The Power of Intention*.

LOVE LETTERS

Looking for love? Here's an idea: Write a couple love letters.

First, write a little letter describing your ideal Love (whether it's an ideal boyfriend/girlfriend/spouse or ideal kid/parent, or ideal business partner or whatever). Go gonzo on the details about the kind of person with whom you'd love to be in relationship. Get it all down.

Got it? Sweet.

Now, time for the much more important part.

Write another letter describing who YOU need to be in order to create and sustain a relationship with that extraordinary individual.

(Note: This letter should be at least twice as long as the first one.)

MUSTERBATION & SHOULDING ON YOURSELF

Wayne Dyer has a great word: "musterbation"—which describes the fine art of doing things because you (insert whiny voice here) *"have to."*

It's kinda like Tony Robbins's idea of "shoulding on yourself"—you know, when you *"should do this and should do that and it's all should, should, should."* His perspective: Do something or don't do it, but quit shoulding on yourself. It's stinky.

So, how about *you?* You musterbating and shoulding on yourself?

Remember: Lovers of wisdom do *nothing* reluctantly. If anything is worth doing, let's do it with all our hearts!

SHOULDS —> COULDS

Speaking of "shoulding" on your self, Louise (founder of Hay House) Hay has a great Idea here as well.

She tells us to pay attention to how often we're dropping the should bomb and see if we can swap out those stinky shoulds with a more empowering "could." (She doesn't quite put it that way, but you get the idea... :)

Feel into this: If I say, "I *should* have gone to that party" or, "I *shouldn't* have said that" there's a much more disempowering energy to it than if I swapped out that should with a could. Like so: "I *could* have gone to that party" and, "I *could* have chosen to not say that."

Can you feel the difference there? It's strong. The "should" implies you're basically an idiot and you totally screwed up while the "could" carries a much more empowered, "Well, yah, I *could* have done it differently, maybe next time I will" mojo with it. Yah?

So, if you're excessively shoulding you might wanna try out the should —> could swapping game!

It's fascinating to see how often the shoulds come out and a lot of fun to see how easy it is to slide into a more empowered perspective.

DON'T TAKE IT PERSONALLY

A lot of teachers talk about the importance of not taking stuff personally.

Marcus Aurelius has my favorite gem.[45] He basically asks us: Why in the world should we care what people, who don't even like *themselves*, think of us?!

Think about it for a moment. The people who tend to get *most* pissy and critical and all up in their stuff about how much they dislike us/something we're doing, tend to be the ones who most strongly dislike themselves.

So, why, oh, heavenly why should we give a poop what they think of us if they can't even form a positive opinion of themselves?

Exactly. We shouldn't. So let's not.

---

45 Here's the passage from Aurelius' classic *Meditations*: *"The approval of such men, who do not even stand well in their own eyes, has no value for him."* Check out the PhilosophersNote for more goodness.

DON'T TAKE IT PERSONALLY
PART DEUX

D on Miguel Ruiz talks about this Idea as well. In fact, it's the second of his Four Agreements: Don't Take Anything Personally.

Why shouldn't we take anything personally? Because what someone thinks of us in any given moment says a lot more about *their* state than it does ours. In Ruiz's words: "Nothing other people do is because of you. It is because of themselves."

Let's think about it. Imagine interacting with the same person in two different situations.

In the first scenario, the person had an AWESOME day—they slept nine hours, landed a promotion at work and won the lottery. They're feelin' great. How do you think they're gonna treat us? Probably pretty well, eh?

Now, same person. This time, they had a really bad night of sleep, lost their job, had a car accident and didn't eat all day long. Not in such a good mood. How do you think they're gonna treat us now? Prolly no where near as well as when they're rested, happy and all that jazz, eh?

The important thing to note here is that WE were exactly the same in both situations. But if we base our opinion of ourselves on how someone else treats us, we're in trouble.

P.S. Countless other teachers talk about this as well. Deepak Chopra encourages us to remember the power of this wisdom with a little mantra: *"I am totally independent of the good or bad opinion of others."*

"I am totally independent of the good or bad opinion of others. I am totally independent of the good or bad opinion of others. I am totally independent of the good or bad opinion of others. I am totally independent of the good or bad opinion of others. I am totally independent of the good or bad opinion of others. I am totally independent of the good or bad opinion of others. I am totally independent of the good or bad opinion of others. I am. . ."

Ahhhh. . . Try it out. It's quite refreshing. :)

INK BLOBS & EMPTINESS

While we're on this whole subject of not taking things personally and the fact that what other people think of you says more about them than anything, how about a couple more Ideas to really bring the point home?

First, ink blobs. Ever heard of Rorschach tests? Basically, psychologists can sneak a peek into their patients' consciousness by asking them to describe what they see when they look at a picture of an ink blob. Now, there's *nothing* *in* the ink blob (other than blobbiness), but what the patient *says* they see tells us a lot about what's going on inside their little noggin.

Second, emptiness. It's a Buddhist concept that basically says everything is empty of meaning—everything is inherently NEUTRAL (kinda like that ink blob). The meaning we give to any particular empty/neutral experience is often an unconscious expression of how we see the world. So, if I'm a pissy person, I'll interpret a neutral event negatively; whereas, if I'm a happy person, I'll interpret that same event in a more empowering way.

Now, the cool thing about this whole emptiness business is the fact that, given the inherent "emptiness" of any given situation, every moment has a "hidden potential"[46]—we can train ourselves to CHOOSE the most empowering perspective.

And, ultimately, that's what it's all about, eh?

Ink blobs and emptiness. Good stuff.

---

46 Geshe Michael Roach describes this *brilliantly* in his great book *The Diamond Cutter*. Check it and my PhilosophersNote out!

FINGERS & LECTURES

Please extend your pointer finger and shake it as if you're lecturing someone—saying something like, *"You shouldn't do this, this and this! Do that, that and that!"*

Thank you.

Now, look at your hand and count how many fingers are pointing at the person you're lecturing and how many fingers are pointing back at you.

Unless you're missing a digit, you should see one finger pointing at the lucky recipient of your wrath and THREE fingers pointing back at you.

You may want to pay attention to that the next time you're lecturing someone.

It's a *really* handy way to notice our "shadow"—the stuff we haven't integrated in our own lives that, unfortunately, we tend to project onto others.

Debbie Ford[47] encourages us to "attend our own lectures" because, more often than not, whatever lecture we're giving someone else is the one WE desperately need to attend.

Try this on: The next time you start telling someone all the things you think *they* need to start doing more of or less of or whatever, imagine you're a student diligently taking notes on the lecture you're giving.

You might just find that the lecture you're giving *them* is what YOU most need to hear!

(And, btw, the sooner you actually do the stuff you're lecturing other people about, the sooner you'll stop lecturing them about it. ;)

---

47 Check out Debbie Ford's great *The Dark Side of the Light Chasers* for a bunch of Big Ideas on how to integrate your shadow (and, of course, my PhilosophersNote on it features some of my favorites!).

HOW AM I THAT?

Speaking of shadows, another *really* powerful way to deal with that dis-integrated murky stuff we project onto others is this little game I often play:[48]

Think of someone who recently annoyed you. Identify what it is about them that *really* bugs you.

Are they greedy? Hyper-ambitious? Impatient? Do they cut people off in mid-sentence and never really listen? Do they act like they know it all?

What is it about 'em that gets you all wound up? Got it? Sweet. Now, ask yourself: *"How am I that?!?"* :)

And make that a practice. What you'll notice, if you're like me, is that we tend to be most annoyed by people who are demonstrating qualities that we are still working on.

Debbie Ford says it's kinda like having electrical sockets on our chest. If we've recognized and accepted our own greed/selfishness/impatience/whatever, it's as if we've put one of those child-proof covers over the socket and no one can "plug into" that energy—we may notice a certain quality in people but we're no longer *triggered* by them.

BUT, run into someone who demonstrates qualities we *haven't* integrated in our lives and yikes! They "plug into" that open socket and we get all pissy.

Again, the solution is (relatively) simple: Notice when you're being super critical of other people and know that you're just observing something within YOU that you need to address. Then celebrate the opportunity to grow as you count how many fingers are pointing back at you, attend your own lectures, and ask: *"How am I that?!"*

---

48 Got this awesome little game from the great book *The Power of Full Engagement* by Jim Loehr and Tony Schwartz. As always, check out the PhilosophersNote and the book if you're feelin' it!

WHOSE BIZ ARE YOU IN?

Byron Katie tells us it's never a good idea to be in God's business (why would we think we should be able to control an earthquake or a flood?) or in other people's business (why would we think we should be able to control a partner or a boss?).

So, let's stay in our own business. It's the only place we can get some good work done.

RAT POISON

Pema Chödrön tells us that being mad at someone and holding a grudge is kinda like eating rat poison and thinking the rat will die. Not very smart.

So, uh, are *you* eating rat poison?

Let go of the grudge, yo!!

A GOLDMINE OF GOLDEN RULES

Ah, The Golden Rule. Shall we mine the virtually identical ethical gems from various wisdom traditions?

"And if thine eyes be turned towards justice, choose thou for thy neighbour that which thou choosest for thyself." — Bahá'í *(Epistle to the Son of the Wolf, 30)*

"Hurt not others with that which pains yourself." — Buddhism *(Udana-Varga)*

"Teacher, which is the great commandment in the law? Jesus said to him, You shall love the Lord your God with all your heart, and with all your soul, and with all your mind. This is the great and first commandment. And a second is like it, You shall love your neighbor as yourself." — Christianity *(Matthew 22:36-40)*

"Tzu-kung asked, 'Is there a single word which can be a guide to conduct throughout one's life?' The Master said, 'It is perhaps the word 'shu.' Do not impose on others what you yourself do not desire.'" — Confucius *(The Analects)*

"This is the sum of duty: do naught to others which if done to thee would cause thee pain." — Hinduism *(The Mahabharata)*

"No one of you is a believer until he desires for his brother that which he desires for himself." — Islam *(Hadith)*

"A man should wander about treating all creatures as he himself would be treated." — Jainism *(Sutrakritanga 1.11.33)*

"A certain heathen came to Shammai and said to him, Make me a proselyte, on condition that you teach me the whole Torah while I stand on one foot. Thereupon he repulsed him with the rod which was in his hand. When he went to Hillel, he said to him, What is hateful to you, do not do to your neighbor: that is the whole Torah; all the rest of it is commentary; go and learn." — Judaism *(Talmud, Shabbat 31a)*

"One [who is] going to take a pointed stick to pinch a baby bird should first try it on himself to feel how it hurts." — Nigerian proverb

"Whatever is disagreeable to yourself do not do unto others." — Zoroastrianism *(Shayast-na-Shayast 13:29)*

P.S. Let's not forget The Platinum Rule. As per Tal Ben-Shahar: *"Why the double standard, the generosity toward our neighbor and the miserliness where we ourselves are concerned? And so I propose that we add a new rule, which we can call the Platinum Rule, to our moral code: 'Do not do unto yourself what you would not do unto others.'"*

"When nature has work to be done, she creates a genius to do it."
— Ralph Waldo Emerson

"Don't ask what the world needs.
Ask what makes you come alive, and go do it.
Because what the world needs is people who have come alive."
— Howard Thurman

"Then the time came when the risk it took to remain tight in a bud
was more painful than the risk it took to blossom."
— Anaïs Nin

"Anything may be betrayed, anyone may be forgiven,
but not those who lack the courage of their own greatness."
— Ayn Rand

"Here's to the crazy ones.
The misfits. The rebels. The trouble-makers.
The round pegs in the square holes. The ones who see things differently.
They're not fond of rules, and they have no respect for the status-quo.
You can quote them, disagree with them, glorify, or vilify them.
But the only thing you can't do is ignore them.
Because they change things. They push the human race forward.
And while some may see them as the crazy ones, we see genius.
Because the people who are crazy enough to think
they can change the world, are the ones who do."
— Apple

EN*THEOS

Spirit. God. Divine Intelligence. Universal Mind. Whatever you call that ineffable force that beats our hearts and keeps the planets in line, it's a (very) good idea to align with it. When we do that? God (theos) is within us (en) as we shine with a radiant enthusiasm that lights up our world!

BEING IN INTEGRITY
VS. DISINTEGRATING

As you might have noticed at this stage, I'm a big fan of living in integrity with our highest values.

Here's another way to look at it: We're either *in* integrity or we're *dis*integrating.

When we violate our own deepest truths it's like we're literally breaking down from within. Eek.

So, remember: Be in integrity. Or disintegrate. The choice is ours, moment to moment to moment...

THIS TEMPLE HAS NO WALLS

Genpo Roshi has a great line about the fact that we need to tear down the temple walls and see the whole world as our monastery/church/synagogue/ yoga studio/dojo/meditation center/philosophy class/ whatever as we see every moment as another opportunity to practice our spirituality.

LOVE. THAT.

And, for whatever reason, whenever I think of this idea I remember my dad (God bless you, Popsicle!) yelling at slow drivers on the way out of our church's parking lot. Even as a kid that always struck me as odd.

These days it's becoming more and more clear to me just how easy it is to check the *"Check me out, I'm spiritual!"* box by showing up for our required # of yoga classes/sitting for our required # of meditation minutes/going to our weekly Holy Day service/[insert-your-"spiritual"-activity-here] and then being a total butthead the rest of the week. Huh? Makes no sense.

Here's to tearing down the temple walls and seeing our entire lives as the practice.

EN*THEOS LIGHTHOUSES

Joseph Campbell once asked: *"What am I? Am I the bulb that carries the light, or am I the light of which the bulb is a vehicle?"*

I say: *"Both!"*

And I think that question provides the perfect metaphor for us to understand our role in the process of connecting to and expressing the Divine within us.

From my perspective, it seems pretty obvious that our job—and our Highest Goal—is to see just how much God we can get flowin' through us in this precious hero's journey of ours. Just how brightly and consistently can we shine our light of creativity and joy and love and kindness and generosity and appreciation and radiant enthusiasm out into the world?

Now, we can be a 20-watt bulb that flickers, sometimes plugged in, sometimes unplugged and bound to blow up if a huge amount of energy goes thru us. Or, we can be a 1,000-watt lighthouse bulb that's unwaveringly plugged in to the highest within us that shines with a radiant enthusiasm that guides our community to their Highest Selves.

It's up to us. I say we plug in and shine.

THINK ARETÉ –
THE MANIFESTO

What would you do if you weren't afraid? OK… So… Uh… What *exactly* are you waiting for?

This isn't a dress rehearsal…

Wake up!

Here's the deal: What we *can* be, we MUST be. Period.

There's no getting around that one. So, turn off the TV. Put down your drink. Get off the medication. Quit numbing yourself. The pain's not going away. Not until you Think Areté.

Think Areté? Yep. Gandhi got it. Einstein got it. Benjamin Franklin got it. Bono gets it. The Dalai Lama gets it. Oprah gets it. And the Greeks definitely got it.

Get this: Guys like Socrates, Plato and Aristotle said that if you want happiness you better live with Areté— a word that literally means virtue or excellence but has a deeper meaning, something closer to "living at your highest potential moment to moment to moment."

Areté. It was one of the highest ideals of Greek culture. It should be one of ours. Tragically, it's not.

We seem to be more interested in resumes, accolades and 401k's.

Speaking of retirement... Who came up with *that*? Work our asses off doing something we're not passionate about so we can accumulate enough money to pay the bills from our stress-caused illnesses while we bitch about what we should have done when we were still young.

Hmmm... Can't quite figure that one out. Seems like it makes a bit more sense to go ahead and dare to live now.

Why not Think Areté?

Live at your highest potential—moment to moment to moment. Not in the mood? Fine. Then live with regret, anxiety, and disillusionment. Your call.

Think about it. When do we feel most alive? Exactly.

When we're being ourselves—our highest selves. You want happiness?

Think Areté.

Live. Love. Smile. Hug. Laugh. Dream. Do. Create. Have fun. Be intense. Be audacious. Be unreasonable. Act impeccably. Breathe. Be you. Be different. Be patient. Get paid to do what you love. Dance in your underwear on your way to work. Why not?

Ditch the tie. Escape the cube. Leave the 8-5. Trash the resume. Ignore the critics and the cynics. Burn the corporate ladders. Laugh at the ceilings. Quit the bitching. Open your mind. End the laziness. Overcome the fear. Transcend the conditioning. Why not?

Move the world. Change the world. Push the human race forward. Whatever you call it, go out and do it.

When? Now.

Not when you have enough money or once you do this or do that. That's nonsense.

It's not gonna be easy, but go out and live your dream.

Now. You deserve it. And, if that doesn't move you: The world deserves it.

Think Areté.

MY TOP 50
BOOKS

Here's a quick look at 50 of my favorite optimal-living books. From old-school classics to modern self-development, tap into the **wisdom that matters.**

OLD-SCHOOL CLASSICS

Letters from a Stoic **by Seneca** – Seneca was born around the same time as Jesus and was one of the leading figures of the Roman Empire. He was also one of history's leading Stoic philosophers (along with Marcus Aurelius and Epictetus). Big Ideas: The purpose of philosophy, the importance of focusing our attention and the mojo we get from facing our fears.

Meditations **by Marcus Aurelius** – Aurelius was a 2nd-century Philosopher & Emperor of the Roman Empire. *Meditations* is a collection of journal entries he wrote to himself. Big Ideas: The importance of never confusing ourselves with visions of a lifetime all at once, not worrying about what others think of us and living a life of purpose and service.

Rumi Daylight **by Rumi** – Rumi was a 13th-century Sufi mystic and Professor of Religion who lived in Konya, Turkey, which was the capital of the dominant Seljuk Empire. His poetry is stunningly beautiful. Big Ideas: The importance of having patience, seeing challenging times as God's way of strengthening us, working hard and going for it.

The Analects **by Confucius** – Confucius was a 6th-century sage from China whose wisdom formed the basis of the philosophy known as Confucianism. Big Ideas: The importance of being a passionate (and patient!) student of life while striving to do our best. Good stuff.

The Bhagavad Gita – The classic text of Hinduism starring Krishna counseling the reluctant warrior, Arjuna. Big Ideas: The importance of meditation, the fact that making mistakes is an inherent part of our growth process and the über-importance of letting go of our attachment to results.

The Dhammapada by Buddha – The Buddha was rockin' it in India about the same time Confucius and Lao-tzu were sharing wisdom in China and not too long before Socrates hit the scene in Greece. A core text of Buddhism, *The Dhammapada* literally means "the path of truth and righteousness." Big Ideas: Living our dharma as we develop self-mastery.

The Enchiridion by Epictetus – Epictetus was a former slave who became a leading Stoic philosopher of his era (1st/2nd century of the Roman Empire). Big Ideas: If we want to be happy, we've gotta realize the only thing we have control over is our response to a situation.

The Selected Writings of Ralph Waldo Emerson – Ralph Waldo Emerson is a hero of mine (he occupies the Great-Great+ Grandfather slot in my spiritual family tree) and his essays, although written in 19th-century prose, totally fire me up. Big Ideas: Self-reliance (trust yourself!!!), the power of enthusiasm, God will not have his work made manifest by cowards.

The Tao te Ching by Lao-tzu – Lao-tzu was a 6th-century Chinese philosopher and his *Tao te Ching* is the core text of Taoism. Big Ideas: Letting go of attachments, gracefully rolling with the flow of life, the journey of a thousand miles begins with the first step (heard that before, eh?!).

Thus Spoke Zarathustra by Friedrich Nietzsche – 19th-century Nietzsche was said to deliver his philosophy with a hammer and this book definitely nails his disdain for conditioning and conformity. Big Ideas: The überman, our worst enemy is often inside our own heads, and pushing ourselves to discover how far we can go.

POSITIVE-PSYCHOLOGY CLASSICS

Authentic Happiness **by Martin Seligman** – Martin Seligman is essentially the father of the Positive Psychology movement. Big Ideas: Using our Signature Strengths consistently throughout our day-to-day lives, moving from a job to a career to a calling as we live a life of meaning and purpose.

Emotional Intelligence **by Daniel Goleman** – One of the classics of Positive Psychology, Goleman's *Emotional Intelligence* established the fact that IQ doesn't account for why some of us succeed and function well and others don't. Big Ideas: The power of delaying gratification, how worrying can create self-fulfilling prophecies, other tips on building EQ.

Flow **by Mihaly Csikszentmihalyi** – Along with Seligman, Csikszentmihalyi is one of the founding fathers of Positive Psychology. *Flow* is all about the science of optimal human experience. Big Ideas: What the flow state is and how to live in it (hint: be fully engaged in an activity that matches your skills with your challenge), controlling the contents of our consciousness to relieve anxiety and boredom.

Happier **by Tal Ben-Shahar** – Ben-Shahar taught one of the most popular classes in Harvard University's history and this book captures the essence of his class on Positive Psychology—sharing the best of what we scientifically know about how to create happier, more fulfilled lives. Big Ideas: The importance of having goals AND living in the moment, going for it, gratitude, happiness rituals.

Happy for No Reason **by Marci Shimoff** – Shimoff created *Chicken Soup for the Woman's Soul* and integrates inspiring stories about happy people with scientifically established ways to boost our happiness in this fun book. Big Ideas: The practice of happiness, set points, ANTs, gratitude, kaizen.

Man's Search for Meaning by Viktor Frankl – Frankl was a leading 20th-century psychologist who survived the horrors of the holocaust and describes his Logotherapy in this classic book. Big Ideas: Our attitudes determine our happiness, *no one* can ever take away the freedom for us to choose our response to any given situation.

Motivation & Personality by Abraham Maslow – Maslow tells us, *"What one can be, one must be!"* (Love that.) He was a 20th-century humanistic psychologist who defined the hierarchy of needs and studied the most exceptional people of his era. Big Ideas: The self-actualizer and the 19 characteristics that make them rock.

The Gifted Adult by Mary-Elaine Jacobsen, Psy.D. – Jacobsen is one of the world's leading authorities on gifted adults and this book is packed with wisdom on how "everyday geniuses®" can rock it. Big Ideas: How to develop our evolutionary IQ as we work hard, silence the (inner and outer) critics and learn how to bounce back as we become co-creators in liberating our everyday genius.

The How of Happiness by Sonja Lyubomirsky – Lyubomirsky rocks. People often ask me what *one* book I would recommend they read. I never had an answer I felt good about until I read this book. It's amazing. The most comprehensive and readable look at what we *scientifically know* works to boost our happiness—from gratitude and exercise to optimism and kindness. Big Ideas: 12 hows of happiness.

The Pursuit of Perfect **by Tal Ben-Shahar** – Another from Ben-Shahar who tells us it's time to quit being perfectionists and start being optimalists. Big Ideas: Looking to our ideals as guiding stars rather than distant shores, embracing constraints, the importance of rest, the platinum rule.

The Six Pillars of Self-Esteem **by Nathaniel Branden** – Branden is easily one of the most articulate human beings I've read and is one of the world's leading experts on self-esteem. Big Ideas: Six pillars of self-esteem—from the practice of living consciously, accepting ourselves and taking responsibility to practicing self-assertiveness, living purposefully and developing personal integrity.

20TH-CENTURY CLASSICS

A Joseph Campbell Companion **by Joseph Campbell** – Campbell occupies the Grandfather slot in my spiritual family tree. This book is an incredible collection of some of his most inspiring wisdom. Big Ideas: Following our bliss, embarking on a hero's journey, being willing to break some eggs to make omelets (aka, making mistakes as we grow!).

As a Man Thinketh **by James Allen** – Although somewhat obscure, Allen was a wise guy and his essays have deeply influenced many of today's leading teachers. Big Ideas: "Dreams are the seedlings" of our future realities, strengthening the power of our minds to live an extraordinary life of meaning.

How to Stop Worrying and Start Living **by Dale Carnegie** – Dale Carnegie was one of the creators of the modern self-dev movement and if you've ever worried more than you'd like, you'll dig the book. Big Ideas: Importance of rest (did you know our hearts rest way more than they work every day?), making decisions and taking action!

Love **by Leo Buscaglia** – Buscaglia was a 20th-century professor at the University of Southern California who taught a class on Love. Big Ideas: If we want to master love, we've gotta *study* it, a truly loving relationship is one in which both partners are committed to their own growth and supporting their love's growth.

Spiritual Economics **by Eric Butterworth** – Butterworth was a 20th-century Unity minister and this book really transformed my relationship to money. Big Ideas: Our goal shouldn't be to make money/acquire schtuff but to achieve the level of consciousness through which abundance flows, true meaning of affluence, security and prosperity.

The Book of Understanding **by Osho** – Osho's a fascinating 20th-century iconoclastic teacher. Big Ideas: Zorba the Buddha, the importance of self-discipline, the fact that we need a firm hold on our ego before we have any hope of letting it go (big point a lot of peeps tend to miss!).

The Fountainhead **by Ayn Rand** – Rand was an über-smart and intense 20th-century philosopher, author and creator of Objectivism. Big Ideas: Our responsibility to own our greatness and to not live as a second-hander (someone who is overly concerned about other people's opinion of them) as we love what we do and know what we want.

The Magic of Thinking Big **by David Schwartz** – Schwartz tells us we've gotta think big if we want to live big. Big Ideas:

Kicking the dreaded "excusitis" disease and developing our "stickability" as we make a compromise with perfection and take action.

***The Power of Your Supermind* by Vernon Howard** – Although he's sold millions of books and his wisdom is strong, Howard is pretty obscure today. Big Ideas: The cause of psychic spankings (codeword for suffering :)), detecting negativity is actually a very positive thing.

***The Wheel of Time* by Carlos Castaneda** – Castaneda was a popular teacher focused on the shamanistic wisdom known as Toltec. Big Ideas: Transcending our conditioning as we develop personal power, the importance of choosing a path with heart, using death as an advisor and living with impeccability as we achieve no-stress success.

MODERN CLASSICS

***Constructive Living* by David Reynolds** – David Reynolds is the leading Western authority on Japanese psychotherapies and this book is a brilliant blend of East and West. Big Ideas: How to live with greater self-mastery by more effectively relating to our emotions and consistently asking ourselves: "Now what needs to be done?!" Best book you've probably never heard of.

***Do You!* by Russell Simmons** – Who knew the Godfather of hip-hop was also an incredible yogi and spiritual teacher?!? Big Ideas: Importance of having a powerful vision for our lives, the fact that a mantra is literally a "tool of thought" we can use to shape our minds, how important it is to take the next baby step as we give ourselves most fully to the world.

Everyday Enlightenment by Dan Millman – Dan's *The Way of the Peaceful Warrior* changed my life and he is one of my favorite teachers and deepest influences. He's also a *really* good guy. This is his magnum opus where he walks us through "The Twelve Gateways to Personal Growth." Big Ideas: Importance of discovering our self-worth (and how to do so), the fact that, although "Carpe diem!" sounds good, it's impossible to do. We can't "Seize the day!" but we *can* "Seize the moment!" Or, as Dan says: "Carpe punctum!" :)

How to Think Like Leonardo da Vinci by Michael Gelb – Michael Gelb is a creative genius in his own right (juggler/speaker/author) and profiles the seven attributes of da Vinci's genius in his great book. Big Ideas: "A Hundred Questions" exercise literally shaped my life, the power of affirmations (did you know da Vinci used them?!) and the body of a genius (did you know da Vinci was also an exceptional athlete?!). Fun stuff.

Integrative Nutrition by Joshua Rosenthal – Joshua Rosenthal runs a nutrition school my Goddess attended and this is a great, grounded health/nutrition book. Big Ideas: Importance of Primary Foods (Joshua tells us that our spirituality, career, exercise and relationships are far more important than what we eat—when's the last time you read *that* in a nutrition book?), the power of following the basics rather than following the latest fad diet.

Loving What Is by Byron Katie – Byron Katie is best known for the four questions that make up "The Work." Big Ideas: Learning to love what is by seeing our suffering as a compassionate alarm clock awakening us to our possibilities and by recognizing that if we see things as "wrong" in the world, we need to start by changing our own consciousness.

***Mastery* by George Leonard** – George Leonard was an author, aikido master, former head of Esalen and all-around awesome guy. This is an incredible book. Super short. Powerful. Big Ideas: How to live a life of mastery, the alternative paths, society's all-out war against mastery and how to win the battle.

***Overachievement* by John Eliot** – A relative of T.S. Eliot and a long line of Harvard presidents, Eliot is an award-winning professor of management, psychology and human performance who's worked with everyone from NBA teams to business leaders. Big Ideas: How to develop a Trusting Mindset where you just let it rip as you eat stress like an energy bar and put yourself on super pilot.

***Spiritual Liberation* by Michael Bernard Beckwith** – Beckwith runs the Agape International Spiritual Center in Los Angeles and is one of the most plugged-in human beings I've ever seen. Big Ideas: Importance of discipline (which becomes blissipline), avoiding spiritual constipation by PRACTICING what we study, how even enlightened beings burn their bagels on occasion (so we can prolly relax into our own imperfections :)).

***The 7 Habits of Highly Effective People* by Stephen Covey** – Stephen Covey's classic has sold 15 million copies and was the first self-development book I read back in the day (1995 to be precise). Big Ideas: Importance of being proactive (huge!), beginning with the end in mind, putting first things first, thinking win/win, seeking first to understand, synergizing and sharpening the saw. All about character development.

***The Alchemist* by Paulo Coelho** – Paulo Coelho is one of the most inspiring and beloved authors on the planet (can you believe he's sold over 100 million copies of his books in 150 languages?!?). I've read and loved all his books. *The*

Alchemist is a super inspiring weekend read guaranteed to kick-start your dreaming. If you like this, check out *The Warrior of the Light* and *Veronika Decides to Die*—two other favorites of mine.

The Four Agreements by Don Miguel Ruiz – Don Miguel Ruiz's classic book on Toltec wisdom has inspired millions. Big Ideas: The four agreements: 1. Being impeccable with our word; 2. Not taking things personally; 3. Not making assumptions; 4. Always doing our best.

The Monk Who Sold His Ferrari by Robin Sharma – Robin Sharma is one of the top leadership coaches in the world and an all-around awesome guy. This book is a fable about a hard-charging attorney who becomes a yogi and shares his wisdom with his former protégé. It's packed with goodness. Big Ideas: The "7 Timeless Virtues of Enlightened Living," the importance of blueprinting our ideal lives as we express the greatness that is our birthright.

The Other 90% by Robert Cooper – Newsflash: You're only using 10% of your potential. Max. Good news is Robert Cooper has a lot of awesome Ideas on how we can rock the other 90%! Big Ideas: The power of syntropy (entropy = a tendency for things to break down whereas syntropy = the tendency for things to perfect themselves), lighthouses (know your values and be a lighthouse, not a weathervane) and other such goodness.

The Power of Full Engagement by Jim Loehr and Tony Schwartz – Loehr and Schwartz tell us we've gotta manage ENERGY not time if we wanna really optimize our lives. Great stuff. Big Ideas: Why we want to be more like sprinters rather than marathon runners, that there's a pulse of life and we need to honor it, and the power of positive rituals.

The Power of Intention by **Wayne Dyer** – I love Dyer and this book rocks. Big Ideas: Floatation wasn't discovered by contemplating the sinking of things (and how you've gotta focus on what you WANT if you wanna see it come to life), how to "act as if" (and not be a weenie about it), how kindness releases the same drugs pharmaceuticals pump into antidepressants (so get your fix by being kind!) and a lot of other great stuff.

The Power of TED* by **David Emerald** – David Emerald's wonderfully wise fable rocks. Big Ideas: The importance of stepping out of DDT (the Dreaded Drama Triangle) and stepping into TED (The Empowerment Dynamic) as we learn to more consistently live from a Creator's perspective (rather than a Victim's) and learn how to hold the tension between our ideals and our current realities by taking baby steps.

The Seven Spiritual Laws of Success by **Deepak Chopra** – Deepak is great and this is easily one of THE most transformative books I've ever read. Big Ideas: All seven spiritual laws including #7 (The Law of Dharma) that inspired me to sell my former business and, eventually, create PhilosophersNotes. (Here's the question Deepak asks that rocked my world: If you had all the time and all the money in the world, what would you do? ... So, what would you do?)

The Success Principles by **Jack Canfield** – Jack Canfield, the creator of *Chicken Soup for the Soul*, gives us a book packed with Big Ideas on the fundamentals of success including: An awesome exercise on how to discover our purpose, the importance of taking responsibility in our lives (that's Principle #1!!!), becoming an inverse paranoid (think: "OMG the universe is out to help me!!" :)), and recognizing that 99% commitment to something is a bitch and 100% is a breeze.

P.S. If I could only recommend 10 books, I'd recommend these potential life-changers (based on their overall goodness + their wisdom to fluff ratio):

1. *The Alchemist* by Paulo Coelho

2. *The How of Happiness* by Sonja Lyubomirsky

3. *The Seven Spiritual Laws of Success* by Deepak Chopra

4. *Happier* by Tal Ben-Shahar

5. *The Pursuit of Perfect* by Tal Ben-Shahar

6. *Mastery* by George Leonard

7. *The Power of TED** by David Emerald

8. *Constructive Living* by David Reynolds

9. *A Joseph Campbell Companion* by Joseph Campbell

10. *The Four Agreements* by Don Miguel Ruiz

P.P.S. Plus: Get "More Wisdom in Less Time" at www.PhilosophersNotes.com where we have 6-page PDF + 20-min MP3 + 10-min PNTV summaries on all these titles + 50 other awesome classics.

THANK YOU

It's impossible to personally thank all the incredible people who have supported me in the creation of my life/this book but I'm excited to give a thank you and a virtual hug to a number of you.

First, my momma. Thank you for teaching me the importance of living with integrity and giving my gifts to the world. I love you and appreciate you.

I want to thank all of my friends and investors who have believed in me, supported me and bet on me. Sir Kanuth, Mr. Bischke, Dave: In addition to being three of my biggest supporters, you're also three of my biggest inspirations. Thank you for being you and for believing in me so deeply. Christiana & Sam & Cheryl, DK, Jessica, LeBaron, Fish, Jonathan, Gary, Michael, Shawn, Beth, Adam & Travis, Rick & Kris, Aunt Bev, David & Barbara & Steve, Joe & Judy & Co: Thank you!

I want to thank John Mackey. You inspire me to live my ideals and to create cool businesses that make a difference. Thank you, sir.

I have so much appreciation for all the authors and teachers who have so passionately explored and shared their truths—Dan Millman, Paulo Coelho, Deepak Chopra, Wayne Dyer, Ken Wilber, Robin Sharma, Tal Ben-Shahar and countless others. Few things give me as much joy as spending time with your wisdom. Thank you for shining your light so brightly and inspiring me to do the same.

All my fellow Philosophers—from Facebook to en*theos: You inspire me. I'm honored to share our lives and I'm giddy to grow together in the months and years and decades ahead!

And, of course, my wife, Alexandra. I love you and appreciate your radiance, your amazing presence and playfulness, your laugh, your smile, your goodness and your commitment to living your most authentically awesome life.

And a quick shout out to the team who helped bring this book to fruition: John: Well done! I'm excited to work and grow together and appreciate all your mojo and good (make that extraordinary) heart! Jacque: So excited to play together and appreciate your enthusiastic support and editorial mojo. (And, Pilar: You're awesome. Thanks for the connection and for being so all-around-amazing!) Rasheeda & Brian: Thanks for your design-fu! M2 & Tripp: Thanks for being the first to read the book and offer such positive feedback!

With a big smile and a heart filled with love: Thank you thank you thank you!!

MORE GOODNESS FROM BRIAN

PhilosophersNotes – From old-school classics to modern self-development, get "More Wisdom in Less Time" with 6-page PDF + 20-min MP3 + 10-min PNTV summaries of 100 optimal living books.
www.PhilosophersNotes.com

Optimal Living 101 – Think of Optimal Living 101 as the class we never had. In 20 classes over 10 weeks, Brian explores the 10 Principles in more depth to help us create our most authentically awesome lives.
www.OptimalLiving101.com

Blissitations – Meditation is powerful. With guided meditations, visualizations, affirmations and other goodness for your consciousness, we help you turn your meditation into Blissitation!
www.Blissitations.com

en*theos – An online oasis for Goddesses and Philosophers to connect with other inspired peeps.
http://we.entheos.me

... AND FROM BRIAN'S WIFE, ALEXANDRA:

Rock Your Goddess Life – Get your Goddess on with a 100-day program all about rockin' the 10 Goddess Elements: Nutrition, Movement, Play, Purpose, Relationships, Sensuality, Confidence, Self-care, Beauty and Spirituality.
www.RockYourGoddessLife.com

BRIAN JOHNSON

loves wisdom. He also loves creating cool businesses that inspire and empower peeps to create their most authentically awesome lives.

MORE AT

http://BrianJohnson.me